The Ride:

How to Ride Your Bike from San Francisco to Los Angeles Without Even Dying

Russell Mendivil

Cover Photo: Day Five, somewhere between Santa Maria and Lompoc

"The Ride: How to Ride Your Bike from San Francisco to Los Angeles Without Even Dying," by Russell Mendivil. ISBN 1-58939-869-6.

Published 2006 by Virtualbookworm.com Publishing Inc., P.O. Box 9949, College Station, TX 77842, US.

Manufactured in the United States of America.

To my wife Laurie
Who believes I can write a book
and pretty much
believes I can do anything…

Table of Contents

October 18, 2004

Thus far I have ridden 1,500 miles to train for AIDS/LifeCycle® 4. Yesterday I registered and trained with many veteran riders. I think I have some work to do, as on some of the up hills, they were singing, and I could barely pant. I think I sounded like an elephant doing Lamaze breathing. I'm glad I started training early.

That was my original training journal posting on my AIDS/LifeCycle® homepage. In reality, I had so much more to say.

I signed up for this ride to pay a debt. I know you can't really make a deal with God, but because of an accidental exposure, I found myself in the position of waiting for the results of an AIDS test for my daughter. In my own mind, I decided if the results were negative, I would do something really big as payback.

The wait was horrific. For the first time, my family and I came across a fear so terrible, we couldn't even talk about it. I knew it was there, and my wife knew it was there, and it hung so thick in our home I'm surprised we were able to move about. But as if we were afraid to "jinx" it or something, nobody talked about the impending outcome.

i

Finally, we got the negative results (she's been tested since with the same results). I don't think I even wanted to admit to myself just how fearful I had been.

It all came out when I went to see "The Laramie Project." It was a very emotional time anyway. Gwen Araujo, a transgender teen, had been murdered in our town, and we were all still in shock to think something so horrific could happen in our own little piece of the world. In a chilling coincidence, our local high school was already rehearsing the "Laramie Project," a play which depicts the aftermath of the murder of Matthew Shepard, a young gay man, in the town of Laramie, Wyoming.

At one point in the play, a mother talks about her child's AIDS test outcome, and she cries when she learns the results are negative. That's all it took for me. I don't think I've cried like that since I was six years old. I'm talking about some serious "sup- supping" here.

As fate would have it, in May 2004, I began cycling with a friend. He had a mountain bike, I bought a nice used comfort bike, and we had some fun little rides. I began riding more and taking on greater distances. Eventually, I began to toy with the idea of an organized ride. I was looking for a good charity ride. It's impossible to go to the Internet looking for a fundraising bicycle ride, and avoid seeing the AIDS/LifeCycle, a 585 mile trek from San Francisco to Los Angeles. There it was, as if God were whacking me on the side of the head with a brick and reminding me I had a major dept to repay.

Logically, and even spiritually, I really don't believe you can make a deal with God. It's not like I believed God was going to smite me if I didn't do the ride. On the other hand, there's nothing wrong with saying a big "thank you" when things go well, and if I could benefit some of my fellow beings at the same time…well then, all the better.

But I felt really funny about signing up for the ride. The ALCers all seemed so young, and for lack of a better term, "hip." They all seemed to know each other, know The City, and know all about cycling.

I was 47 years old, I didn't know a soul involved with ALC, and I'd only been riding for five months. I'd had two heart attacks. I'm pretty much a big old chubby couch potato kind of guy. My kids say I look like "Hispaniclause," a Mexican Santa. I loved the indentation my tush had worn into my recliner chair in front of the television.

Besides, most of the ALC people seemed to be training out of San Francisco. I felt like a foreigner whenever I visited The City. I was always lost and confused. Everything always seemed so big, crowded, and overwhelming.

Then I discovered an ALC discussion forum and wrote an entry entitled "Is it normal to be this afraid?" A host of people answered my question, but the first reply came from Derek. He wrote:

> *There is a first time for everything. Look round the site and all the different posts. You are not alone in your angst. It isn't a gay ride, so it doesn't matter if you're straight, gay, bisexual, transgendered, pre-op, post-op, in a dress, slacks, kilt, or shorts. It doesn't matter whether you are White, Black, Asian, American Indian, Hispanic, Middle Eastern, etc, ad infinitum. It doesn't matter if you are a carnivore, omnivore, or herbivore. It doesn't matter whether you ride a borrowed twenty year old beach cruiser, a ten year old hybrid, a six year old road bike, or something that just hit the showroom floor. Just get great tires and put your bike and your body in top condition. Fear? It is the element of emotion most*

commonly encountered. Working your way through it is part of the whole journey. Just start now, and know that you are never alone.

Before I did my first training ride, which was to be on the same day I signed up for the ride, I again inquired on the discussion forum, and was comforted by a Training Ride Leader, Julie Brown. She told me she would be one of the TRLs for the ALC Northern California kick off ride, and she would make sure I was okay.

On October 17, 2004, I summoned up all my courage and walked in the door of the Sports Basement at the Presidio in San Francisco. I was about 45 minutes early. As I fully expected to get lost on the way, I had allowed plenty of time.

I anticipated a large crowd, so I thought they might have cancelled due to the inclement weather, because it had been raining all night. I waited a bit and was about to give up and leave when I saw a small group of people. One man was wearing a watch cap with an ALC logo. He apparently noticed I looked lost and smiled warmly. I asked if he knew where I signed up for the ride and he introduced himself as George Harrison.

Derek was right. From the moment I spoke to that man, I have never been alone on this journey. I was so close to leaving, and if I hadn't seen George, I'm sure I would have, and likely wouldn't have had the guts to try again. I would have missed out on so much! I can hardly believe the people I've met, the places I've been, and the things I've seen and done. And I owe it all to the AIDS LifeCycle®.

It's funny how I tried to pay a debt, and just ended up owing more. It's just like credit cards!

There's no doubt that one of the most defining moments of my life was my first heart attack, and yet, I couldn't say exactly when it happened. I know it was late August, 1997, but I can't give you an anniversary date, and I don't celebrate the day as my rebirth or anything like that, though I might if I knew the date. That way I could have a second birthday party each year, and get twice as many gifts.

When you tell people you've had a heart attack, they always ask you if it was "a bad one." I always want to say, "Oh no! I'm one of those lucky guys who had a 'good' heart attack, and it made me thinner, wealthier, and better looking."

I know what they mean to ask is "How serious was it?" The answer is, about as serious as a heart attack.

My first myocardial infarction (what the doctors call it) limited the functioning ability of my heart and changed my life forever. The second was a minor reminder to live a healthier lifestyle. Still, if you were to tell someone you had Cancer, would they ever ask if it's bad?

I do remember during the couple of weeks preceding my diagnosis, I was exhausted and wanted to rest all the time. I had what felt like really bad indigestion that just wouldn't go away. Finally, when I had pain so bad that it literally dropped me to my knees while I was working, I began to think, "Hmmm… maybe this isn't indigestion."

So I went to the Doctor, or more accurately, a nurse practitioner. After a few questions and a couple of tests, it was determined that I had…indigestion. They sent me home with a prescription for Tagament. A day or so later, I called to tell them the Tagament wasn't working because the chest pain continued. They told me I hadn't even given the medication a chance to work, give it a few more days and stop drinking coffee.

The pain continued to increase for another week, and I began having horrible pain in my jaw. I decided to go to the dentist. I told him my woes, but he couldn't find anything that would cause jaw pain. He did give me a prescription for the pain though, and while my heart and jaw continued to hurt, thanks to the Vicodin, I didn't care about it so much.

Finally, after a week of ever-increasing pain, I went back to see a different doctor. Dr. Winslow Wong took one look at me and sent me to "the special room," where they immediately put me on oxygen, and transported me by ambulance to the hospital.

To make a long story (possibly my next book) short, I had an angioplasty, and it was very successful. I spent a lot of time whining about "Why me?" I talked about it with my cardiologist, and I told him I didn't know one other 39 year old that had had a heart attack, and his response was "That's because they're all dead!"

So I whined a bit less. In retrospect, it's amazing I lasted so long *without* a heart attack. I always tell people the base of my food pyramid at the time was rocky road ice cream. I smoked nearly two packs a day for 25 years. I was 65 lbs. overweight.

I felt I owed my best shot for a complete recovery to my wife Laurie, and my three daughters, Erin, Megan, and Katelyn, who were 15, 13, and 11 at the time. I quit smoking, and I lowered my cholesterol significantly. But when I quit smoking, I gained weight rapidly. A year before the ride, I was 87 lbs. overweight. I began to look for exercise options.

Laurie and I started walking. Walking proved difficult for me because I'm a gardener, and I pretty much walk all day long. Usually my feet and legs are ready for a rest after a hard day at work. Walking eventually gave way to an elliptical machine. As long as I was listening to music I almost enjoyed it. And then one day, a friend of mine invited me on a bike ride.

I thought I had a bike, and so I accepted. But when I went home to my back yard, I found what I really had was a rusted pile of garbage. I began looking for a "new" bike.

I bought my first bike on May 8, 2004, Mother's Day. Okay, it wasn't my first bike, but it was my first since I had purchased a Schwinn Varsity in seventh grade. We were having a big get- together at our house, but I was determined to get this bike, as it was an exceptionally good deal. As it turned out, I bought a matching pair, one for myself and one for my wife (Happy Mother's Day!) from a couple in Los Gatos. I know buying your wife a bike for Mother's Day isn't cool, and I'm sure I got her something else before then, but now she even likes the bike.

Because it was Mother's Day, and because I was already under scrutiny as I left Mother's Day morning to buy a bike, I was only able to ride the bike four blocks that first day, and even at that my butt was sore. It was a beautiful bike, a silver 2002 Specialized® Expedition, a hybrid comfort bike with an upright sitting position and fat comfy tires. My wife's matched, but was smaller and forest green. I paid $120 for the pair.

I liked riding. Somehow it made me feel like a kid again. My rides increased, both in frequency and distance. I have some great trails about two miles from my house, and I spent a lot of time riding the Alameda Creek trail, and Coyote Hills Regional Park. I nearly always rode alone.

I saw some amazing things. I developed a real appreciation for the birds and other wildlife I encountered. I remember one evening I had a near miss with a skunk on a trail at Coyote Hills. Another evening I had a race with a fox, as it was running parallel to me. I had a really nice time scouting out trails I hadn't yet ridden. I'd ride an hour or two almost every night.

Before long I was beginning to wonder about distances, and how far I could go. I'd ride as much as 27 miles in an evening, and on the weekend I could ride 35 miles. I didn't know anything about hydration, or nourishment. I did take water bottles, because I got thirsty, and that much only made sense.

I broke 50 miles one day on a ride to the four corners of our neighboring city, Fremont, which is, I've heard, the second largest (square miles) city in California. I did another fifty-mile ride to Shadow Cliffs Regional Park in Pleasanton.

Then one day I decided to try for a metric century (62 miles), just riding the Alameda Creek trail back and forth. At this stage, it was all about the miles, and I never rode hills. All was well until about the fifty mile mark, but I was so close to my goal, I just kept riding. The more I rode, the more difficult it was to do anything at all. By mile 54 I was disoriented and cramping up everywhere. I was "bonking" or "hitting the wall," but at the time I didn't know what was happening to me. I rode straight home, about two more miles, but it was a tremendous struggle, and I had to stop and rest a couple of times in that two miles.

Medically, I think bonking means your blood sugar level has gotten low because your body has been depleted of glycogen. Whatever the cause, bonking was a really horrible feeling. I was confused, weak, and miserable, and it was not something I'd care to repeat.

Generally speaking though, I was really enjoying my cycling. I wanted to take it to the next level, and I noticed all of the folks that were as old as me, or as fat as me, but much faster than me, had bicycles with skinny tires. I figured it would speed me up to have a bike with thinner tires, but I wondered how much.

I wasn't ready to go with a bike with the traditional ten-speed look, with the bent handle bars, but I found Specialized made a hybrid bike with skinny tires, upright seating, and straight handle bars. I bought a used Specialized Sirrus for $275. To me, this was serious money for a bike, and I had buyer's remorse almost immediately. Still, I was beginning to consider a benefit ride of some kind, and I knew I would need a faster bike.

I got a flat tire the first two times I rode the Sirrus. I hadn't yet learned fat tires will take a lot more abuse than those little thin tires. I resolved this problem by avoiding gravel roads, and also by buying a puncture resistant tire called an Armadillo, by Specialized. I've since learned there are many such tires on the market.

But I was a faster rider now with my skinny tires, by about two miles per hour, which would be no big deal if I rode 30 mph. I, however, had been averaging 12 mph with the old bike, and was up to a blazing 14 mph with the new bike.

The first time I took my new bike into my local Specialized bike shop, the owner really bad-mouthed it. I don't know if he was just trying to sell me a more expensive bike, or if he just had a serious dislike for the Sirrus. He did have me test ride a Specialized Sequoia, and it was love at first ride. The Sequoia Elite, my dream bike, sold for $1,200. Where I come from, $1,200 will get you a decent car.

By now I was toying with the idea of doing AIDS/LifeCycle 4. I'd heard of the ride, read about it in the paper, and seen past participants on the news. I began researching ALC on the Internet. It seemed like an impossibly lofty goal.

The AIDS/LifeCycle is the official cycling event of the San Francisco AIDS Foundation and the Los Angeles Gay and Lesbian Center. The ride was to take place June 5-11, 2005, and would entail riding 585 miles, from San Francisco to Los Angeles. The event was designed to raise awareness and knowledge about HIV/AIDS among participants, their donors and the general public, while at the same time, raising funds for the beneficiaries, so they might continue their lifesaving work in the community. Each participant is required to raise $2,500.

I'm not the kind of guy who normally goes in for adventure. I went on a river-rafting trip when my wife was pregnant with our first daughter, twenty-five years ago. Since my wife and I began rearing children, my biggest quest has probably been the Jungle Ride at Disneyland. I'm a pretty mundane "Dad" type of guy.

Younger, stronger, and yes, thinner riders with better hearts do ALC on all kinds of bikes, including mountain bikes, hybrids, comfort bikes, and even tandems and recumbents. But I knew if I had any chance at all of doing this ride, I would need a great road bike.

I began searching Craigslist, an Internet want ad bulletin board, hoping to find a used Sequoia at a reasonable price. I was almost obsessed with the idea that if I looked hard enough, I could find a great deal. Finally one day, I found a couple in Hollister who were selling two 2003 Sequoias for $750. I had my own little cash stash, and I borrowed more cash from my daughter Megan. I headed straight for Hollister, which is almost a two hour drive from my home. I purchased both bikes, and with a bit of work, I was able to sell one of the two for $675 the next week. I had my dream bike for $75! This was the first of many signs that made me believe ALC was my destiny.

The new bike was awesome, but I had one problem. It came with these "fancy-schmancy" racing wheels with fewer spokes than a regular wheel. Initially I thought it was just because I was 65 lbs. overweight (even after losing 22 lbs.) that I kept breaking spokes, but after some research, I found this was a common problem with these wheels. I'm sure, though, that the extra weight didn't help matters any.

By September 2004, I think I'd read everything available about ALC on the Internet. I was riding 15 miles on a route that included the Dumbarton Bridge several times a week, and I was regularly doing at least 35-50 miles one day each weekend. I had also discovered an ALC discussion forum on the Internet. In my mind, I had already committed to do the ride when I made the following post on my Mom's birthday, October 5th of 2004:

Two questions for you all:

Is it normal to feel this afraid? I have only been riding since May, and am up to about 100 miles per week. I have never done an organized ride, but I am going to the Kick Off ride on the 17th, and I'm registering for the ALC.

But I am so nervous. I'm middle-aged, overweight, and oh gees, straight! I don't know a soul involved in the ride, and perhaps even worse, I don't live in SF or Berkeley. Will I be welcomed and accepted? I'm not even a vegetarian!

And will I be able to do the mileage? How can anyone do 585 miles in seven days? My longest ride is 57 miles and it took me two days to recuperate.

The second question is will my bike make it? I have a used 2003 Specialized Sequoia Expert but the spokes break, and then the wheel bends and it's worthless until I get the tire trued. Can I just buy a bunch of spokes and carry them with me? Can I make the bike rideable until I can get to a mechanic? Or should I just get new wheels? What kind?

I am bound and determined to do this ride...but I am scared and it's only October. What am I gonna be like in June. And oh yeah! A tentmate? In my whole (adult) life I have never slept in a room with anyone but my wife. What if I snore in my sleep...OR WORSE?

Maybe my wife could be on the crew. We could make a new movie and call it "Ma and Pa Kettle do the ALC...Oh gees!

The response was pretty overwhelming. The first was from Derek, but there were many more. Riders not only responded on the forum, but e-mailed me as well. The clincher for me came from a man who I've since learned is an ALC celebrity. Bert Shaw was the oldest rider on ALC 4. He was 77 years old at the time:

I think it is normal for someone in your situation, yes. But, you are doing fine by riding 100 miles per week at this point.

I know I was quite hesitant when I signed up for my first ride, in 2003. I had a serious cycling accident in June of 2001 and as a result I was limited to riding a recumbent tricycle. I had spent four months in bed and was using a cane to get around and had been riding my trike for only a few months. But I was determined to do as well as I could. I trained well, (except for enough hills) and as time went on my confidence increased. Living in Santa Barbara I had limited access to training rides so I was mostly on my own, but I kept at it.

And yes I am straight and was 75 years old on my first ride. I found the riders and support people to be among the finest I have met anywhere. They are all dedicated to your success on the ride. I rode every day and covered about 480 of the 585 miles, not bad. I had trouble on the hills which meant I had to do more hills in training for my next ride, ALC3. And this in spite of five flats and several mechanical problems.

ALC3 was more fun, I knew what to expect, the hills were shorter and less steep, at least it seemed that way. I started earlier each day as I know I am slow and wanted to finish, which I did, most days. With new tires and more road vigilance I had no flats. I secured each adjustment screw with LokTite and so, no mechanical problems, not one.

You will learn that your body is a marvelous organism and if you train well you will find that each ride is easier, that you are stronger and your endurance better. It's just the way things are.

I am now training for ALC4 and will be 77 when I ride. I am doing more hills and will be in the best shape of my life when I finish.

So, take heart, train well, and you will have the time of your life.

As to your bike, I suggest you get the opinion of an expert. One thing I know is that the ride is enough of a challenge that you don't want to be dealing with poor equipment, even though there are helpful bike techs about every 20 miles at every rest stop.

9

Best regards,
Bert Shaw no 5191

If Bert could do it at 77, after recuperating from a serious accident, then so could I. At least that was my reasoning.

Nobody ever addressed the "tentmate" issue, which was a very real concern for me. ALC riders are required to either pick a tentmate, or have one assigned to them. I would feel horribly uncomfortable sleeping in an 8'X 8' tent with any man. I think a lot of other men will understand that. And to be quite honest, I couldn't imagine finding a woman with whom I would be comfortable sharing a tent, let alone my wife being comfortable with the idea. It was a bridge I would have to cross when I came to it.

I had made the commitment to go to the Kick Off Training Ride, and register for ALC4 on October 17, 2004. I used to hate driving in San Francisco. I mean it when I say I felt like a foreigner there. They drive really differently in the city, as opposed to my little Newark, CA. So just getting to the place to sign up was a scary prospect for me.

After a nerve-wracking drive, I was going to have to jump into a group where nearly everyone knew everybody else, and I would be a complete stranger. Being the stranger in a large group is never a fun proposition for me.

Then after the uncomfortable initial meeting, I would go on my first training ride. I'd never ridden with more than one person before. I didn't know if I could keep up, or if there were hills involved and how steep they were. I was terrified. That was my state of mind when I walked into the Sports Basement at the Presidio in San Francisco. And that's how I was feeling when I spotted George Harrison.

The Sports Basement is a converted army commissary. It is a huge store with every conceivable kind of sports equipment and apparel. I have since learned they are a huge supporter of the AIDS/LifeCycle as well as other community causes. They also have some of the nicest employees I have ever found, and some of the best bike techs you will ever need.

The weather was drizzly, it had been raining all night, and I was trying to talk myself into believing they had just cancelled the thing. If they cancelled, I could just go home and watch the rain from my window and snuggle up with my wife. I could be safe, warm, comfortable, and everything I wasn't feeling at the Sports Basement that morning! I was headed out the door when I saw George in his ALC watch cap. I think he knew I was lost right away, and asked me if he could help me with anything. I asked him if he knew where I signed up for the ride, and he said to wait with him, and he'd find out.

George has a very soothing voice, and his calming demeanor had me almost settled by the time I left him. He showed a genuine interest and caring and he asked why I was doing the ride. Not wanting to go into too much personal detail, I just answered "It's a good cause." I felt like an idiot as soon as I said it. Nobody rides 585 miles for a cause they think is crappy! Sheesh!

Of course George agreed with my profound statement. He's such a good guy. He chatted with me for a bit, and eventually led me to Susan Parish, who signed me up in between the million other tasks she was handling.

Susan was kind, but very busy, and while I was hanging around because I didn't have anywhere else to go, I realized she had other things going on. I stepped away, and for a while just watched as everyone hugged and asked about friends and family.

I finally figured out everyone knew everyone except three of us; a red headed guy who introduced himself as Jeff, a really pretty young lady with a blue Cannondale bike named Kelsey, and myself.

I called them both over to the center of the group and told them this is where the people who don't know anyone stand.

They took me seriously, and for a while the three of us introduced ourselves and chatted.

Before too long I found Julie Brown, or Julie found me. I don't remember which, but she probably noticed me first. I told her I would be easy to identify, as I'm the big scary Mexican guy. My daughter's band instructor once picked me out of a crowd along a parade route using that description alone. However it happened, Julie greeted me warmly with a handshake and a hug. Julie is a tiny Filipino woman. She's pretty, and energetic, and right away you can tell she has a wonderful heart. Almost immediately, Julie introduced me to Shelly Ross, who both literally and figuratively took me under her wing.

Shelly's taller than I am, and she has the warmest smile you'll ever see. She put her arm around me, and gave me a squeeze and a look that said, "Stick with me kid and you'll be fine!" Shelly is a good ten years younger than I am, but she made me feel as though she was my big sister, and she would keep me safe from harm.

Then a young man whom I later found out was my first "Cycle Buddy," Derek Martin, talked about the wet roads, the risks associated with them, and the ride that day. As soon as you sign up for ALC, a Cycle Buddy is assigned to you to help you with any questions you might have about training, fundraising, or any other ride related topic. Derek was my first, but when he got promoted, a young woman named Josie Chapman replaced him. I asked them all my questions by e-mail, and they both answered incredibly quickly. They have both been wonderful support!

Derek said it had been decided that they would cancel the longest ride, which would have been 50 miles. It was the ride I had planned on doing, as I had ridden 50 miles before. This turned out to be a real stroke of luck, as my flat 50 miles, and their hilly 50 miles designed for a mountain goat, are two very different things.

Derek asked how many of us had been over the Golden Gate Bridge before. I've lived in the Bay Area all my life. Of course I've been over the Golden Gate Bridge! I raised my hand immediately, as did nearly everyone else. I was smugly thinking to myself, heck, I've even walked across the Golden Gate Bridge! And then it occurred to me. Could this guy possibly mean "How many of you have been over the Golden Gate Bridge *on a bicycle?*" And so I asked "Do you mean on a bike?" The crowd roared with laughter. Someone said, "You'll fit right in here!" They all thought I was joking, but I was dead serious. It didn't matter, as long as I was fitting in. I played it off as though I was just a really funny, quick-witted guy, as I sheepishly pulled my own hand down, using my other hand for emphasis.

Derek said the conditions were very difficult today, and novices shouldn't take the ride to Sausalito. He told us there was a sweeping downhill on the other side, and it was dangerous when wet. I really wanted to ride over the Golden Gate Bridge, and take the longer ride (what was I thinking?) and I tried to convince him by telling him I rode the Dumbarton Bridge almost daily. Derek didn't give his blessing until Julie Brown told him "I know this guy. He'll be fine."

She pulled me aside and said "Trust your gear for the downhill" and I thought it was a reference to down-shifting my bike down the hill and riding in a lower "gear," and then it occurred to me that this was just stupid, because you can downshift 'til the cows come home on a bicycle, and it won't slow you down one bit. So I begged her pardon, and again she said, "Trust your gear" like it was a Jedi command or something. *"Feel the force Luke and trust your gear."* But Julie Brown doesn't look that geeky, so I asked once more, and as it turned out, it was a question. Did I trust my gear for the downhill? Bike, brakes, tires etc.? I told her I did.

Then a Training Ride Leader named Bob Katz called us all together, introduced us to himself and the other TRLs that would be participating in this ride, Julie Brown being among them. He then took us through a ritual that was so strange to me at the time, but which by now is almost as familiar as the Catholic Mass.

He led us in some stretching exercises. These were all very foreign to me. Everybody else seemed to know what they were doing. Shelly was off to the side, doing her own stretching exercises, ignoring our leaders. I didn't know who to follow, so awkwardly I tried to do both.

Then Bob gave a safety speech which I though was overkill, but I soon found out it was mandatory before any training ride.

Ride defensively and always stay alert. Always assume cars drivers don't see you, assume drivers underestimate your speed, obey all traffic laws, especially stop signs and traffic lights....don't be under the influence...all riders must wear a helmet...ride single file...no headphones...no drafting, always leave one bike length between you and the next rider...call out "on your left" when passing, and always pass on the left...call out objects on the road such as "glass," "pothole," or "grate"...signal when stopping or turning (he demonstrates signals) or call out "slowing" or "stopping"...notify other riders if a car is passing, by calling "car back," and point out and call out approaching traffic "car right" or "car left."

I wrote all of the above from memory, so perhaps I've missed something, but over the course of my training, those TRLs obviously taught me something. At the time though, I thought I'd never remember any of what Bob said.

With that we all walked over to our bikes and started off. The riders were a sight to behold, clad in jackets and jerseys of every bright color imaginable. Watching them, I was excited; but to be a part of them, I was thrilled!

"Clipless pedal" is a term I will never understand. I think it's used because the term "toe clip" was already used for those little baskets you stick your toes in on bike pedals. It gets confusing, because when you lock your foot into a clipless pedal, it is described as "clipping in." Therefore, one "clips into" a clipless pedal. It's kind of an oxymoron, like "congressional ethics" or "military intelligence." At any rate, you know your cleat is clipped into your clipless pedal, because it makes a distinct "click" when you do it.

I was nervous as hell as we started off, but I have to tell you, when those fifty or so riders all clipped in together; that "click-clicking" was one of the most exhilarating sounds I had ever heard!

The adventure was about to begin...

October 18, 2004 Training Journal Entry

Thus far I have ridden 1,500 miles to train for AIDS/LifeCycle 4. Yesterday I registered and trained with many veteran riders. I think I have some work to do as on some of the uphills, they were singing, and I could barely pant. I think I sounded like an elephant doing Lamaze breathing. I'm glad I started training early.

Shelly stayed with me through every inch of that first ride. She taught me so much that day, about cycling, about "The Ride," about sticking with it. Shelly is an awesome teacher; she is patient, and caring, and sometimes pushy, and I will always consider her my cycling mentor and Godmother. If you could pick a sponsor in ALC, Shelly would definitely be mine!

Right after the "big click," Shelly called out for me to follow her, which I did, straight to the second and third spot in the long line of riders. I knew there was no way I could keep up with the pack leaders, and I was very worried until Shelly explained, "I like to start out at the front of the pack…it makes people feel good when they're passing me."

I handled the small hills up to the Golden Gate Bridge fairly easily. Riding over the bridge is a joy. When you drive over the Golden Gate in a car, it creates a beautiful picture for you with the bridge, the fog, the ocean, the sailboats, the pedestrians, and the cyclists. But when you ride over the bridge, you're a part of it. You're *in* the picture.

If I thought going over the Golden Gate Bridge was a pretty great thrill, the downhill after the bridge to Sausalito was exhilarating! My knuckles were butt white from squeezing my handlebars so tightly. The term "butt white," was given to me by my children when they were in the lower grades of elementary school. It helps to understand the term if you know I'm Hispanic and my wife is white, and we live in a very culturally diverse community. One of my daughters was trying to get a second daughter to remember a fellow classmate:

"What color hair does she have?"
"Brown/black" was the answer.
"Is she white?"
"Yeah"
"Brown/white? Like us?"
"No! Butt white like mama.

I was having the time of my life riding down that monster hill, that is until I realized I would have to climb back up the hill on the return trip. Derek Martin was right about the hazardous wet downhills, but it had stopped raining for some time now, and the roads were dry, but for a few puddles that could easily be avoided.

I'd never been to Sausalito before. It's a beautiful little town with an incredible view of The Bay. I've since ridden through perhaps a dozen times. I never tire of the view and the ambiance, and I always wish I could stay longer.

Our pack regrouped at Mike's Bikes, a bike shop in Sausalito that I've since learned is another big supporter of the AIDS/LifeCycle. I have needed help from these folks several times while on training rides, and they go out of their way to give assistance and get me or my fellow riders back on the road quickly.

We then rode on to a coffee shop in Mill Valley. We stopped for muffins and coffee. Julie and Shelly both commented they were part of the "ride to eat" club. As we dismounted, I was shocked by the casual way all the riders just leaned their bikes against a wall or pole, and then walked into the shop. Nobody locked a single bike, and I thought to myself, "You're not home in Newark anymore." These bikes wouldn't last five minutes against the wall at the police station in Newark. I was somewhat hesitant to leave my bike there, but when I looked around at the other bikes leaning all over the place, my used $75 bike looked mediocre at best.

Shelly and I snacked together. We talked about my wife and my family a bit, but mostly she talked about the ride, and I never grew tired of listening. Shelly is truly dedicated to the cause, and a real asset to the ALC community. She was great company too, and I hoped this would be the beginning of a lasting friendship.

Before long, some of the riders began the trip home. Shelly and I finished up, and headed back as well. The ride was scenic and uneventful until we reached the Sausalito Hill. Shelly calls this "TLFH," or "the last fucking hill." Both Shelly and Julie warned me I might not make this hill on the first try. Shelly said she'd had to walk it the first few times, and the first time she attempted it, she cried. I found it amusing whenever anybody couldn't ride up a hill, and had to walk up instead, everyone referred to it as "cross training."

To give it some perspective, I remember when I first began riding, I considered a freeway overpass a "hill." The Dumbarton

Bridge, which I rode often, was a "big hill" when I first began riding, and the grade was steep enough that I could only manage to keep a pace of about 7.5 mph. TLFH is the "up" side of perhaps 30 freeway overpasses, with maybe a couple of very brief flat sections in the middle to catch your breath. It was everything I could do to keep a pace of 2.9 mph.

The first time I try any hill is always the worst, because I never know how far you have to go, or how much you can push, or how much you need to save for later. That was all pretty much irrelevant on this hill. It seemed it was everything I could do to keep riding, from beginning to end.

Julie rode in front of me, slowing if she ever got more than 30 feet ahead of me, and Shelly stayed behind, encouraging me all the way. They were like guardian angels, and I'll be eternally grateful for their encouragement. Shelly was saying things like "Wow! You're doing it! Just one more big hill!" and Julie began singing "High Hopes."

I was just starting to get into Julie's song when Shelly said "Julie?" Julie kept singing "Just what makes that little old ant think he can..." Shelly again said "Julie!?" Julie kept on, louder now "Cause he had HIGH HOPES!" Now Julie was belting it out like that kid from "Annie!"

Shelly once more said "JULIE!!!" Finally Julie, who I suspect knew all along she had been antagonizing Shelly, asked ever so sweetly, "Yes Shelly?" To which Shelly yelled "SHUT the FUCK UP!!!" I was a bit shocked, and I laughed hard enough that it was difficult to keep pushing up the hill. I almost fell over, but I didn't. Though it was a struggle, I kept right on pedaling to the top of that hill.

I'm sure most people have made it up that hill on the first try. It really doesn't matter, because, for me, it was a great accomplishment and I was so proud I nearly burst my buttons. The rest of the ride was sheer jubilation!

Riding out over the Golden Gate was wonderful, but it was even more magnificent on the return trip. Sometimes when you work hard for something, you value it all the more. That bridge was one of the most beautiful sights of my life. I've ridden it many times since, and it never fails to impress me.

It was all downhill from the bridge back to the Sports Basement, and I was already looking forward to my next ride. As we were completing our trip, the rain that had threatened all morning, began to fall. I was pleasantly surprised to see many of our fellow riders were there to cheer us in. It really made me feel as if I belonged, and that I was really training for AIDS/LifeCycle 4.

10-29-04 Training Journal Entry

I've done about 1,650 miles in training but I've hit a small snag. Okay, not so small. I broke my wrist. Who knew when they made the big "NOT A STEP" sign on the ladder, they meant it was not a step. Go figure? No, really the ladder broke. I'm looking for a trainer, a device on which you place your bike so you can "ride" stationary, and I'll start cross training as well. It's early and there's time to heal, but I don't want to lose too much momentum.

This was no small snag! I was at work trimming shrubs at the top legitimate step of an eight-foot ladder. It was the customer's ladder, and it looked good enough. Ah! But appearances can be deceiving, and termites eat from the inside.

I was trimming for a minute or so when the ladder broke, nay, exploded into maybe fifteen pieces. I was more concerned about getting away from the gas powered hedge trimmer, than my landing. I once filleted my arm with a hedge trimmer, and once was quite enough. I knew the odds of me keeping the trimmer in my hands and away from my body were almost nil, so I threw it as far as I could while I went down, and landed on my wrist.

I knew it was broken before I got up. I called my wife, packed my tools, and as I was leaving, my customer stopped me to ask about other gardening projects. I told him I had just broken my wrist, but he just kept on talking, and finally I walked away as he continued to ramble on. Sometimes being a gardener makes you feel less important than cheese.

The good news was that it was plenty early in the season to quit riding for six weeks and get back in shape. Shelly and I had kept in touch since my first ride, and when I told her I had broken my wrist, she was concerned and supportive. She let me know she had a trainer, she could either loan or sell to me, and I ended up buying it. I worked out on it enough to keep from losing everything I had built up physically. Still, I definitely regressed over the time my arm was in a cast.

11-24-04 Training Journal Entry

I think I lost too much momentum. I got a new cast today that's smaller (had a full arm cast bent at 90 degrees). I can ride again (sort of). I am slower and in worse shape. I can't shift with my left hand, as it is too weak and dysfunctional. I can't ride my road bike at all. Still, riding is riding, and as Gene Autry said on more than one occasion, I'm back in the saddle again.... whoopi-ty-aye-oh...

Autumn is my favorite season. I even like working in the autumn, though the falling leaves can add hours to your work-week when you're a gardener. Still, the air is crisp and clean, and it just feels good! I was sorely disappointed I had missed riding the entire season with my broken wrist.

Working one-handed didn't do much for my earning power as a gardener either. My days were longer, and while I was meeting the minimum requirements of my customers, there were just some things I couldn't do, at times testing their patience.

I certainly wasn't doing any extra work I might normally be doing to get ready for Christmas. All in all, it was a pretty depressing time. Still I tried to remain positive. I had a lovely ALC blue cast that I accessorized with an ALC orange

AIDS/LifeCycle wristband, with the slogan "We Can We Will We Must (end AIDS)."

After six weeks, when I finally got a wrist cast and was able to ride, I was ecstatic!

11-28-04 Training Journal Entry

The AIDS/LifeCycle web page has a training ride calendar which you can visit to choose training rides. It lists such information as date and time, location, ride leaders, miles, pace, climbing level, and RSVP information. Early in the season, there aren't many rides, but by the end of the season, there might be as many as six rides in a single day from which to pick. I chose this one, because the pace was "beginner" and the hill level was "easy."

Today's ride was 32 miles and wouldn't normally have been a challenge, but for two things. First, this is my first training ride since I broke my wrist, and I just got my full arm cast off a few days ago. I was riding in a wrist cast and had only been able to ride again since Thanksgiving, four days ago.

Second, I have no strength at all in my left wrist, so I am unable to shift the left side gears on my road bike, which controls the derailleur on the rear cassette. On my mountain bike I can reach over and pull the left shifter with my right hand, so that's what I rode.

I was able to keep up with just a bit of difficulty. At one point, due to traffic lights, the group split, and somehow (with no idea where I was going and a very poor sense of direction even if I did) I ended up leading a pack. So I followed the lead group at a great distance calling and pointing out obstacles as best I could. "GLASS!" as I rode by a broken bottle gesturing with my hand. "CLEAR!" as I rode slowly through an empty blind intersection. With each hand gesture I made with my right hand, I might as well have been riding with no hands, because as weak and useless as the left hand with the cast was, it was pretty much just coming along for the ride. So I only had contact with the person directly behind me, a cute young girl who didn't look old enough to be on the ride (you have to be eighteen). She was very kind and sweet, and a great conversationalist. I thought she was a pretty nice kid to be so friendly and engaging with this old guy. My "daddy" instincts came into full gear as I was leading this kid and the others on this portion of the ride. We came to a creek trail, and I'm familiar with these, as I spend a great deal of time riding on the Alameda Creek trail. We came to a downhill under an overpass. On the Alameda Creek trail these drops are always followed by steep climbs to get back to level ground. So, as I always do on my local trails, I zoomed down the hill anticipating the grade at the end.

To my horror, the downhill went into a tunnel, and coming out of the tunnel at full speed, I saw not the uphill I anticipated, but a slight decline with a very sharp right turn. I am familiar with the terms to call out when slowing ("SLOWING!") or stopping ("STOPPING!") but I have yet to encounter this situation. Should I call out "SLAMMING ON MY BRAKES TO KEEP FROM FALLING DOWN THAT VERY STEEP HILL!?" Perhaps I should shorten the call to "SAVING MY ASS!" followed up with a "GOOD LUCK!"

By the time I debated this, it was too late. I hit my brakes once, went into an uncontrollable slide, let off, pulled back, slid, let go, pulled once more and stopped, of course forgetting to call out "STOPPING!" I immediately thought to apologize to the cute kid following me. I looked back to see a whole new face, and off in the distance, far behind me now, I saw my new little friend bouncing down the hill.

I missed the first half of the crash, but the second half was spectacular! Did you ever see the film clip of the guy doing the extreme skiing and he falls down the cliff face, bouncing lifelessly as his skis fly off in all directions? Take away the skis, add a bike, divide it by four, change the snow to very long winter grass, and that's what I saw. She finally came to a stop, landing on her knees with a look of shock on her little face. Slowly her mouth began to open and then...she started giggling uncontrollably!? She said it was a very soft landing.

Of course I apologized profusely, and she said it was her own fault. Maybe so, but I am certainly not qualified to be leading any portion of a ride!

Finally, a more experienced rider (a certified Ride Leader), moved to the front of our group, and we finished the ride safely. With the exception of my share of the responsibility for the crashing girl incident, and the ridiculously small size of the éclairs at the fancy coffee shop where we stopped, I was very happy with the ride. I mean, nobody died or anything.

The certified Ride Leader was Sue Lackey. We met first thing in the morning because this was the coldest ride I had ever done, and we all huddled very close together as we listened to the ride instructions and the safety speech. Sue and I stood next to one another, and ended up being stretching partners. Sue was a veteran rider of a few years, and she gave me a new perspective. Like Shelly, she was very dedicated, and she had developed a close friendship with a fellow rider, David, who is HIV positive. I could tell she really cared for David, and so now, for her, the AIDS/LifeCycle had become very personal.

We spent most of the day riding together, and we talked about everything from the ride, to our families, to her job as a teacher. We had a great time and I decided I'd like to ride with her again.

Sue seemed to know everybody on this training ride, and she knew Julie Brown as well. She told me she would be leading a ride after the holidays called "The Three Bears." It sounded intriguing and strangely familiar, and I told her I'd try to be there.

Once the cast was removed, I returned to training in earnest. I tried to ride for one half hour before work, and again after work. As the days were very short, all of my weekday training was in the dark. I always had to ride slower, because my light doesn't illuminate far enough ahead if I'm going any faster than about 12 mph.

It was freezing cold riding in the dark in December. I had purchased gloves, and I rode with a hooded sweatshirt and tights. Any time I had to stop at a traffic light, my glasses would fog up and I'd remove them until I got my speed up again.

It took a great deal of commitment to get started, and I hated the first half mile or so, but once I got going, I loved my freezing cold winter night rides.

2-12-2004 Training Journal Entry

It should be noted this is only my perspective. Others on the ride would probably just sum this up by saying: the fat old guy that slowed us down fell…

I knew it would be a great day for riding, because as soon as I pulled up to our meeting point, someone was leaving a parking space and I pulled right in, delighting at my great fortune.

I haven't been riding so much since I broke my arm on October twenty-ninth, and I am nowhere near the conditioning I was in before the "broken arm/ladder incident of '04." I went on one 32-mile training ride in Concord two weeks ago, where it was mostly older folks, almost my age! It was fairly flat terrain and even though I had to ride my mountain bike, which is slower than my road bike, I did well. I managed to keep up with the pace, though it was difficult at times.

This last week, I rode in San Francisco with a younger group. I was definitely the oldest, by perhaps ten years, and I haven't done any hills since I broke my arm. Also, I am still unable to ride my road bike due to my damaged wrist.

It was a beginner group, but they were all young and strong. As soon as we hit the first hill on Arguello Street, I knew it was going to be a long day! I just couldn't keep up! Everywhere we went, there were more hills.

So it was a twenty-two mile ride, and we stopped to regroup three times. Each and every time, I was the last person in. You know him, the person who gets all the mercy cheers and applause. Yes, each regrouping was a true Special Olympics moment for me. I didn't think I could be any more humiliated, but au contraire!

One of the many beautiful women in the group was riding in front of me (yes that would be in the second to the last position!). While shifting gears, her chain came off. I, of course, white knight on my silver steed, came to her rescue.

To truly appreciate this story, you have to understand that, from time to time, my injured left wrist will twist a certain way and send jolting pain through my arm, which causes it to jerk outward, in a sidearm casting motion.

So as I'm stopping alongside the unchained fair maiden, I unclipped my right foot from my pedal, and began to lean right, to stop with my right foot down. My left foot was still clipped in. However, as I hit the brakes, my left wrist twisted just the wrong way, sending searing pain through my left arm, causing me to jerk it out to the side.

This, of course, shifted my center of gravity to my left side, just as I came to a full and complete stop. Remember now, that my left foot was still clipped in. I tilted to the left and fell, nay crashed, over on my left side. I landed on my already injured left arm causing it to convulse even more violently as I lay sideways on the ground with my bike in the unconventional "lying sideways" riding position.

Have you ever defecated in your pants in a public setting, and it's running down your leg, and smelling horribly, and everyone around you tries to pretend they don't notice even though it's impossible not to notice? Well, Thank God, that's never happened to me, but I do have a new appreciation for just how that might feel, because that's exactly how all my fellow riders, and all those who witnessed this event, reacted.

I believe about 3/4 of the population of San Francisco were present to watch this, though this (and only this part of the story) may be an exaggeration. There they were, all avoiding my gaze, suddenly finding interest in imaginary scenes elsewhere, anywhere but my direction, whistling and hum-dee-dumming.

Even the fair unchained damsel "didn't notice" though my convulsing arm was now slapping at her ankle uncontrollably as I lay on the ground.

The unconventional "lying sideways" riding position is a difficult position from which to recover with the "I meant to do that" hop-step away. I, however, managed a half-hearted attempt, and mercifully, somebody else helped the lady with the errant chain.

We continued on, climbing silently through the hills, with the shared unspeakable horror behind us. I was almost certain it would begin snowing, so we might feel exactly as the Donner party did so many years ago after their rescue.

It was twenty-two miles, and I don't believe we ever came to a downhill. Still, my pickup was parked right where I left it, so I knew we had come full circle. There it was, but now she was adorned with a crisp, new, bright white, $50.00 parking ticket!

On this ride, I met Alan Kwok. Alan is another incredibly supportive and giving TRL, and a friend of Shelly's. It seems Alan is a friend of everyone's though. In fact, I've yet to meet anyone involved with ALC, that isn't a friend of Alan's, and I can understand that. He cares about everyone.

After the ride, Shelly, Alan and I piled in my pick-up and went out for a burger. I was upset with my ride, not thrilled with the parking ticket, and really determined to get thinner and healthier so I could be a better, stronger rider. Yup, right after this burger, I was going to start losing weight!

1-10-05 Training Journal Entry

This is the first journal entry of 2005. For those of you counting, 2005 is the year I'm going to ride my bike from SF to LA. That's this year, and quite honestly, just between you and me, I'm a bit frightened. This ride will be difficult, and the closer it gets, the more I realize I'm really going to do it, or at the very least, give it one hell of a try.

All the other riders say there is no shame in walking up hills if you need to (cross training), or sagging (having them drive you to the next rest stop or into camp) if you can't go on. But everyone knows the goal is to ride, as they so eloquently put it, "EFI" or "Every Fucking Inch." Hey it's not my term, I just reported it. Anyway, it seemed so much easier when I could say "next year I'm going to do that ride.

Thus far in my training I've ridden 1,952 miles. My goal was 2,000 by the end of last year. I was kicking myself because I didn't make it, but the reality of the situation is, had anybody told me in 2003 I'd ride 1,952 miles in 2004, I'd have told them they were about two wheels short of a bicycle. I didn't even do 1,952 miles a year on a motorcycle when I owned one.

This brings me to my latest training ride. Today's ride was called the "Three Bears." It's a ride that started at the Orinda BART station, and ended going up three hills on Bear Creek Road.

My new friend, Sue Lackey, was one of the two Training Ride Leaders. The weather was a bit threatening, but Randy (the other Ride Leader) and Sue determined we were going to go for it. I put my faith in them.

I'm back on my road bike, and this ride was a bit of redemption after the fateful ride of '04. I had no trouble keeping up with the pack. Oh, did I neglect to mention I was, in fact, the entire pack. Yup, Randy was in front, me, and then Sue was sweeping. Still, I felt like I was keeping the pace with no problem, maintaining about 17 mph on the flats.

Then we hit the hills, and Randy was off like a bat out of hell. Sue stayed with me, and she says I kept up with her pace just fine. I don't know if she held back for me, but I made the first hill thinking, in spite of all I'd heard about these "Three Bears," the first, at least, wasn't so tough. So I was feeling pretty darn good, had the old confidence back, and then Sue informed me we hadn't reached the "Bears" yet. In fact, they began about another five miles ahead of where we were.

The rolling hills on this ride, in their winter coat of lush green, were breathtaking. Literally. And they were really pretty too. This was probably the most beautiful ride I've done. Getting to The Bears was uneventful, save for the great conversation with Sue.

Finally we came to the "Three Bears." The Bears were not as difficult as I had imagined. I took them in short order at a sizzling 3.5 mph. Look out Lance! They were seriously long and steep, but I never once considered resting or walking. The downhill was awesome, but what impressed me the most was Sue. You see, when riding in a group we're taught to point out dangerous objects on the road. Riding single file you might hear riders call out "glass" or "grate" or "road kill" while pointing out the object as they pass it. Sue has the most beautiful, graceful pointing gesture I have ever seen. It's a cross between a magician's assistant and a stewardess, but quick and subtle. I can't really define it, but it's uniquely Sue.

So there we are flying down these hills at 35 mph on what I believe are far too skinny tires for a big guy. If you run over a paper clip on the road at this speed, you're airborne. I was hanging on with both hands in my white-knuckled death grip following Sue, and she's still gesturing away. Sorry fellow riders, but if you're behind me at 35 mph, pay attention, because I don't care if I see the Pope lying on the road there, I'm not pointing him out!

So we completed the Three Bears, and I was thinking it was all smooth sailing from there on out, no more hills, when Randy said, "There's one more. Watch out for Goldilocks cause she's a bitch!" She was a minor inconvenience at best (or worst).

Oh yeah, another highlight of the ride was seeing Sue do her little gesture while calling out "Bell Pepper" which she says is a first (what's a bell pepper doing out in the middle of nowhere?)

Perhaps the low point was breaking a spoke...my fourth with these wheels. Randy says I'm just too big (nice way of saying "fat") for these wheels and spokes. I am going to buy new (used but new to me) wheels.

As it turns out, Randy had a pair of Mavic Open Pros he no longer used, and he sold them to me at a very reasonable price. I never broke another spoke.

1-17-05 Training Journal Entry

I broke 2,000 miles today. That's noteworthy to me. I also did some cycling apparel shopping.

Trying on leg warmers was perhaps the most effeminate thing I had ever done in my life. That is until I put arm warmers on with a sleeveless shirt. They look like evening gloves minus the hands.

When I started riding I vowed I would never wear spandex. I cannot believe I have digressed to this point...

Never say "never." There were so many things I said I wouldn't do, to which I eventually succumbed before the ride began. I'd have saved myself some serious cash, had I just accepted the idea that cyclists look ridiculous for a reason.

I resisted a serious road bike, because I thought I'd be uncomfortable riding hunched over on those down-turned handlebars. What I didn't know was most riders spend very little time riding down on their "lowers," and spend the majority of the time in a more upright position with hands on their "hoods," the covering where the brake lever meets the handlebar. I only ride on my lowers when I'm riding into a headwind, to decrease wind resistance.

I thought an upright riding position would be more comfortable for me, and if you're only planning on riding a couple of miles, that's probably true. But if you're riding long distances, the more you lean forward, the less pressure on your butt, and it's the butt that's going to be hurting first.

Although straight handlebars might appear more comfortable than bent bars, I found there are three basic hand positions with bent bars, the straight part of the top of the bar, the hoods, and the lowers. Not only do these three positions allow you to use different upper body muscles, each position changes your seat positioning as well, and while it might only be a slight change, it will be appreciated after 70 miles. Straight bars offer only one position.

The idea of "clipping in" to a pedal, in essence locking your feet into pedals, seemed ludicrous to me when I first began riding. Still it's only logical that if you can pull on pedals as well as push, you'll be a much more efficient rider. Actually, really good riders train themselves to apply even pressure at every point of the pedaling circle.

For me, toe clips, seemed far less dangerous. Toe clips are like little metal baskets you slide your toes in, and they usually have little straps that go over the center of your foot. I bought a pair, and it was a complete waste of money. Within a week I was buying clipless pedals.

Even then, I couldn't commit to clipless. I bought a "campus" pedal. It's clipless on one side, and a regular pedal on the other. But then you have to spin the pedal to the correct position before you finally clip in. Within another week I switched out to full clipless.

There are different types of clipless pedal systems. I chose SPD's (Shimano Pedaling Dynamics) because they seem to be the most universal, and frankly, they were the cheapest. They're actually geared more for mountain bike riders, but I found they worked well for me. I also bought mountain bike shoes because they have a more bendable sole and are easier to walk in once you're off the bike. I bought shoes for about $30.00 on sale at Performance. The cleats, which have to be attached to the shoes, were about $10.00, and the pedals were maybe thirty something dollars. When a friend of mine went clipless, she found a set of pedals and cleats at Supergo for $20.00.

I was certain I would want a second set of brake levers on my bike for the upright position, and I think that was a big factor in my choosing the Specialized Sequoia Bicycle. In reality the brake levers left no room to mount a cycle computer, or a light. I discarded the second set of levers and it took about two days to get used to this. Had the bike never been equipped with them, I never would have missed them.

As much as I resisted riding a road bike, my hesitation was nothing compared with my reluctance to purchasing cycling clothing. I was very happy to ride in shorts and a t-shirt. Eventually though, padded shorts were beginning to sound more appealing. Such was the level of my suffering.

I was really embarrassed to purchase shorts. I had no idea what size to buy, I didn't want to try them on in a store, and you don't wear underwear with them! This is a pretty hard and fast rule, I guess because they'll shift and be uncomfortable. Shelly says they'll rub raw spots into your skin that are unbearable too. I'll just have to trust her on that.

Sometimes on training rides, we use landmarks in the pack to refer to your position in the group at any given time. Obviously, if you know a rider, you might say, "back when we were riding with Bob." But if you don't know a rider, you might say "when we passed the guy on the Blue Cannondale" or "when we stopped at the light by the lady with the long blonde hair."

On one training ride I noticed a lady was wearing underwear under her bike shorts. I thought it was just me, but later, I heard her referenced at least three times by other riders as "the lady wearing the underwear."

Finally, I ordered a pair of the cheapest shorts I could find on eBay. They fit nicely and were comfortable up until about 30 miles. Strangely, I liked them way more than I care to admit.

I was also resistant to cycling jerseys. Let's face it. They're not very figure flattering to a guy who looks like me. I much preferred a t-shirt, even though other riders told me I'd be far more comfortable in a jersey. Jerseys were my last hold out, but when you're riding hard, and sweating profusely, a t-shirt just holds too much moisture. Jerseys "wick" moisture away from your skin, and dry very quickly.

Leg and arm warmers were a must have for me. They're convenient for long rides, because in the morning when it's cold, you have long pants and sleeves, but as the day warms up you can remove them, without having to remove your jersey or shorts. Some riders prefer knee warmers to leg warmers. You can also get toe warmers, or whole shoe coverings.

Leg warmers are simply polyester sleeves for your legs with elastic at the top, and zippers on the bottom. At the top, they tuck under the elastic on the leg of your shorts. The ugliest thing in the world is when the leg warmers drop a bit, and leave a gap between the shorts and the warmers, making it look like a fat old guy with nasty hairy legs is going for that sexy Britney Spears thigh high look.

Finally, I should have purchased a more expensive helmet right up front. It makes no sense to me that the more vents you have on your helmet, which means the less material they use to make said helmet, the more expensive the helmet is. What a scam! Anyway, the more vents in the helmet, the cooler you will ride. My second helmet was so much more comfortable. This was important to me because I've often heard, in many situations cooler heads prevail…ahem…

1-22-05 Training Journal Entry

I went to a training session with Curtis Cramblett today. Curtis is a physical therapist, cycling coach, and strength and conditioning specialist, but lots of folks simply refer to him as "the Bike God." I learned a lot about efficient bike riding...enough to know I'm not. He gave me plenty of things to work on, and also reinforced the idea that a bike fitting would be very beneficial.

After the session, I went for a scheduled training ride with a large group that was a copy of the first training ride I ever did, the ride in which I met Shelly, Master to my Grasshopper, and Downtown Julie.

Today's ride was much easier than the first. While I don't think I am in the riding shape I was in back then, experience is worth something. Shelly and I spent a good deal of the time riding alone together. She was in a crummy mood today, so it was a bit difficult to keep up with her over the Golden Gate Bridge as she let out that negative energy.

After that, it was a beautiful ride...just a bit too windy. I practiced some of the stuff Curtis taught, I listened to Shelly rant and rave (she is so entertaining and colorful, and not just her language either). All in all, it was a great ride, and as we came to the end, it seemed like it was over far too quickly.

This ride was the first time I met a woman named Jeanne McArthur. She was a red-headed, curly haired, attractive, rather intellectual looking woman. She was riding with another blonde woman, also name Jeanne, or possibly Jean. I talked to the two of them at the shop where we drank coffee and snacked. Blonde Jean did all the talking, but they were both very nice, and they rode about my speed. Every time I saw them, they were together. As it turns out, this was just coincidental.

1-23-05 Training Journal Entry

Today I faced my nemesis. This was a repeat of the fateful ride of '04 where I crashed (literally) and burned. They label this ride innocently enough, calling it the "Punch and Pie" ride. But I know the hell it can be...

My daughter Megan, who is an excellent athletic specimen, came with me today. Megan can make anything fun.

This was a glorious comeback! While I wasn't the first guy in, I certainly wasn't the last! The hills were difficult, but not unbearable. I was very happy with my performance after my last defeat there. No Special O moments for me today, no siree Bob!

Megan and I spent a lot of the time riding in a pack with Edna Flores, who gave us Brady Bunch trivia questions as we rode, and Jeanne McArthur, who deserves an honorable mention for her graceful and beautiful hand gestures.

This was a wonderful ride! Thus far I have ridden 2099 miles in my training.

It was great having Megan on this training ride with me! It was nice someone from my family could see what I do with my Sundays, and besides, Megan, like all of my daughters, is a really fun person.

Jeanne McArthur and I spent a good portion of this ride together, and I realized I see her so often because we ride the same speed. I really began thinking about other people with whom I'd ridden, like my dear friend Shelly, and how she always had to hold back or wait for me. It was nice riding with Jeanne, because I was riding at her pace, which was very comfortable for me.

Even better, Jeanne was entertaining, hyper-honest in her stories, and hilarious! We talked after the ride while we ate pie, and I was pretty sure we'd be doing some riding together, though I had no idea how much that would turn out to be.

I also met the Hudson sisters on this ride, Tilmin and Kelly. Kelly appeared quiet, warm and friendly. I had no way of knowing she's really hysterically funny, warm and friendly.

Tilmin was a bundle of energy and made me laugh from the moment I met her. When I asked about a tattoo on the inside of her calf which I later learned was a picture of a fertility goddess, Tilmin said it was a picture of her naked, saying "See? Big boobies, big belly, it's me!"

I always like it when I see adult sisters who are such good friends, probably because I hope my own daughters will remain close as adults. Tilmin and Kelly ride together, live together, and work together.

Like me, Kelly, Tilmin, and Jeanne aren't exactly the thin athletic type. In fact, if you put us in a room with fifty other people, we would likely be the last four anyone would suspect of attempting a 585 mile ride, and no one would ever guess a 30 mile ride is a piece of cake for any of us.

Megan was very comfortable in the group, and she helped serve pie, using the hood of someone's brand new mustang as the table. Megan spilled pie all over the hood, but nobody cared, least of all the car's owner. It was nice having some father/daughter bonding time. I think we both really enjoyed it.

First sheep encounter (Courtesy of Shelly Ross)

Training Journal Entry ...Super Bowl Sunday..... The Sheep Ride!

Originally this was listed as a 51-mile ride from Pittsburgh BART to Los Vaqueros Dam, which, I guess is in Brentwood (I'm not exactly the Ferdinand Magellan of cycling).

It turned out to be 58 miles. About the last seven miles I was thinking the designers of this ride were deceptive and evil. Now, after recuperating and having time to reflect upon it, I think the designers of this ride were deceptive and evil.

Actually this was a truly beautiful ride. Pittsburgh sounds like an awful place, but it's very pretty, and not too congested. The ride only got more beautiful the further we rode, and the closer we came to the dam.

Once we neared the dam, for about the last mile or so, we encountered a huge flock of hundreds of sheep. They made the ride challenging, as once we approached it became a top priority of the lambs to join with their mommies.

I learned something about sheep. Apparently, when they eat, they are like humans at Thanksgiving, having a separate "kids table" (not a goat reference). This became obvious because, originally, none of the lambs were eating on the same side of the road as their moms, and so they dashed in a panic across the road in front of us. It was really wonderful to be a part of this, although I'm not sure the sheep felt the same about it.

Just an aside, as a second year high school Spanish graduate, and a Hispanic, someone should let the folks running this place know "Los Vaqueros" doesn't mean "the sheepboys."

The hills out were rolling and not too difficult, and we had a tailwind all the way. The only really tough hill was an optional detour to the top of the dam, which I foolishly chose to do. I should have known I would need that energy at the end of the ride.

Somewhere on the way back, with more than 20 miles left to ride, I broke yet another spoke (I had not yet installed the new wheels I purchased from Randy). My tire would rub against my brakes with each turn, which does nothing for ones speed or efficiency. At the Starbucks stop, with 15 miles to go, the Ride Leader suggested we remove the back brakes altogether.

I learned something else on this ride...nobody wants to have a big fat guy missing a rear brake riding behind them. Hmm...Who knew?

The bad thing about departing with a tailwind is that you have to ride with a headwind on the return trip. Between the bent rim from the broken spoke (which became progressively worse throughout the ride), the headwind, and the fatigue of doing 58 miles, I really struggled to finish this ride. I came in with the sweep and the last rider, but I finished.

I am only more determined to work harder to be a stronger rider.

While my friend Shelly did this training ride, we rode together only briefly. I rode pretty much alone for the majority of the ride, enjoying Shelly's company at rest stops.

The sweep was a nice guy, and I wish I remembered his name so I could thank him here, but as with the other ride (the fateful ride of '04) where I had such a difficult time, and the sweep was so kind to me, I have no recollection of it. Maybe I tried to block the whole experience from my mind.

I didn't much care for riding alone, albeit in a group, and it wasn't fair to expect Shelly or anyone else to slow down for me. The idea of finding a riding companion that rode at the same speed as I, was beginning to appeal to me and as fate would have it, Jeanne McArthur e-mailed me just about that time.

I sometimes give my e-mail address to people I meet when I'm on training rides, and I always tell them if they ever want to do some riding, to e-mail me. Fortunately, Jeanne was the first to take me up on the offer. We set up a ride for the following Saturday.

2-12-05 Training Journal Entry

Today I cruised with Jeanne. We did 35 miles, from my home, around Coyote Hill's Bay View Trail, up Nike Hill, back to the Alameda Creek Trail, and all the way out to the end of the paved trail at the bay. Then we rode back to the other end of the trail at Mission Blvd., into Historic Niles.

I kept referring to "Historic Niles" and finally Jeanne asked why it was called "Historic" Niles. Her timing couldn't have been more perfect as we were just passing a sign which said "WELCOME TO HISTORIC NILES." I explained it's called "Historic Niles" pretty much because the sign says so.

We toured the park and Shinn Pond, and then we came to the realization we were starving. We decided if you don't want tea, alcohol, antiques, or to get your nails done, Niles isn't the place to be.

We rode back down Mission to Mowry, had a nice lunch at Spoons, and headed home. Jeanne is a fun riding partner and I'm thinking we'll be doing a lot of rides together. The only problem is we need to push each other more, because we got to talking and only averaged a bit better than 11 mph.

No question about it, Jeanne and I rode well together, if a bit too slowly. I was comfortable with her immediately, and I could tell she was with me. We took turns leading, and while I enjoyed riding with other more experienced riders, when I was riding with Jeanne, we were equal partners and I liked that aspect of our riding relationship.

The only danger I could foresee was we might have a serious accident because we made each other laugh so hard! Jeanne is very funny!

2-13-05 - Training Journal Entry

Today we began a CAT II series of rides that are starting at 31 miles, and adding 10% per week, building to our first century (100 miles) in May. It was a great ride, with about 40 people.

I have done the first part of this route three times now, and it is getting easier, so I guess I am improving. The ride starts at the Presidio, and goes through Sausalito, Mill Valley, and into Tiburon. This was my first time going all the way to Tiburon. It was really beautiful!

On the way back, we got caught in the rain, and I realized I haven't ridden in the rain since I was perhaps in Jr. High School. I had forgotten how wet brakes don't stop so well. I'm not the kind of person who normally rides a bike in the rain, but the ride has changed me, even before I've done it. The reality of this hit me when Jeanne decided she would be better off if she removed her pants, which were becoming heavy with the rain. I mean, sheesh! I don't remember the last time I was in a bus stop, on a bike, sheltered from the rain, in Mill Valley, with a lady taking her pants off (yes, she had cycling shorts underneath her pants).

The hill coming in from Sausalito, TLFH, is tough, but it really is getting easier each time. Sure, most everyone passes me, but I'm still riding. I don't think I'm actually going any faster yet, but I'm breathing easier and I don't struggle as much.

We made it back in without much difficulty. In spite of the rain, it was a great ride, and I hope I'll be able to do these CAT II Series Training Rides every Sunday until the Century ride in May!

2,270 miles thus far in my training

All of the official ALC training rides are categorized by speed and terrain. Category 1 through 4 rates the speed of the ride, 1 being slow (8-10 mph), and 4 being the fastest (15 mph and faster). The CAT II series (category 2) was medium paced at 10-12 mph. On this first CAT II Series ride, we ended the ride at Café Acri in Tiburon. There was a group of riders sitting and talking at a table and roaring with laughter. One of the riders was a TRL whom Shelly had told me about, describing her as "hilarious." Stephanie was, in fact, the center of attention at the table, cutting up with a fair-haired, small-framed man I later learned was named Kurt.

As I walked over to introduce myself to Stephanie, Kurt stood up angrily, feigning great offense at something someone had said and spat out, "Look! I may have tendencies, but I am definitely not straight!" Everyone howled.

2-20-05 Training Journal Entry

Today was the second ride in the CAT II series. It was the same as last week, with a very nice loop added through some beautiful homes in the countryside in Tiburon. I love it there, and to think, I didn't even know the place existed before the training rides!

I picked up Jeanne in the early morning, and almost as soon as we were on the freeway we got pulled over by the California Highway Patrol for an expired registration. The two officers took forever, and had virtually no sense of humor. While they were running me for warrants, etc. (because if you look at me, you know I must have outstanding warrants), I called my wife to find out where the new registration sticker might be. When I tried to explain to the officer the new sticker was on our refrigerator, and we certainly wouldn't want to be in violation if we were ever driving our major kitchen appliances about, he only yelled at me to get back in the car.

So, ticket in hand (the third since I started these training rides), I drove on to the Sports Basement.

I was late. I missed part of the safety speech, and was very politely told I could not be part of the training ride. I was very disappointed, but I understand, rules are rules. I was thinking about walking my bike back to my car, when the ride leader went on to tell me that though he couldn't prevent me from joining them, he would have to remove my name from the sign-in sheet, and I would not "officially" be a part of the ride. He asked me for my name, so he could scratch it off the sign-in sheet.

I have no idea why...but that really hurt. I felt like Chuck Conner in the opening of his show "Branded" after he got drummed out of the Army for desertion. Still, my bud Jeanne assured me if I were to get hit by a car, she'd dial 911 for me.

Later, she told me now I could do the rest of the ride with no hands and no helmet, things ALC training ride rules prohibit (see, I have the safety speech memorized). I rode with them...well I kind of slithered along with them. I felt like I should be in the "Naughty Corner" and everyone else should ignore me.

The highlight of the ride was possibly when I looked back to make sure Jane, a lady with a very cute English accent, was still following us. We had assured her she could follow us into the Presidio. I glanced back and she reassured me by saying, "I'm right on your tail...and what a fine tail it is!" That quickened my pedaling a bit.

Even though I wasn't "officially" on the ride, it was a great day with great company!

2,371 miles thus far in my training

So evidently somebody ratted me out! I had gone into the Sports Basement to get a water bottle for Jeanne, because she doesn't pay any attention to the rules, and forgot to bring one. At this point I hadn't yet discovered what a flagrant rule violator Jeanne really is! We knew we were late when we pulled in the Sports Basement parking lot because of those two dawdling cops that pulled us over.

I definitely got the feeling once those CHP officers stopped me, they took one look at me and knew they had something, and I felt like they were horribly disappointed when all they could do was issue a fix-it ticket for my registration. It's not that I'm a cop hater, I respect them, and I'm grateful they're willing to do their job, because I wouldn't do it!

I've now been pulled over 134 times, and I've only ever received two fix-it tickets, including this evil registration sticker infraction, and a red light violation back in 1980, my most heinous crime to date. I think perhaps I just look like a bad guy, though my mom would argue with that.

Once we arrived at the Sports Basement I told Jeanne to grab the bikes, as I figured I was the faster of the two of us, and I ran in to get a bottle, and then of course I had to rinse the bottle out. As I was just beginning to fill it, Edna looked in the door and yelled, "They're starting the safety speech!" I finished filling the water bottle. So in the time it takes to run twenty ounces of water, I became an outcast.

Ben Armstrong, Training Ride Leader extraordinaire, and I had not yet met. Ben's a tall, thin, handsome young man. I'm as straight as they come, but I can see why all the young girls love Ben. He also speaks with a beautiful British accent, and in that beautiful accent he told me, "It has been brought to my attention that you were not present for the entire safety speech."

I told Ben the story of the dawdling cops, and I told him I was pretty familiar with the safety speech. I wanted to start reciting it for him, "Ride defensively and always stay alert. Always assume cars drivers don't see you..." but I knew he had rules to follow, and the last thing I would want to do is make life difficult for a guy that's volunteering his time for such a worthy cause. Still, I felt horribly dejected, and was about to head back to my truck when Ben went on to say "Whilst I can't prevent you from riding the same path as us, I will need your name to scratch it off the sign-in book."

It would never have occurred to me to just go ahead and do the ride with them, even though I'd be riding as an outlaw! With Jeanne's reassurance, and many other riders encouraging me to ride along, I joined them. I am so happy I did. If not I would have never received Jane's ass compliment, and more importantly, gotten to meet Jane.

By the way, the sign-in book is the method by which the TRLs keep track of who started a ride, and then they have a sign-out sheet to keep track of who finished. All riders sign in when they arrive, giving such information as name, rider number, e-mail address, phone number, and time in. At the end of the training ride, they leave a book with sign-out sheets, and you simply sign out with your name and the time. If you fail to sign out, they have to go through the trouble of contacting you so as to insure all riders made it in safely.

3-5 and 3-6-2005 Training Journal Entry Jeanne's Tour and Cat II part 3, SF to Fairfax

Saturday I decided with all this riding I'm doing I needed to avoid a long formal training ride so I could mow my back lawn, which I haven't done since last year. I met up with Jeanne at her place, and immediately we noticed her back tire was low. I also noticed her tube valve was broken. I should have known right then this was an omen for the weekend. Just as quickly as we inflated the tube, it deflated, and simply wouldn't hold air.

I began removing the tire when Jeanne explained you only had to remove half the tire to change the tube, and it worked very well. Then she handed me the new tube, and as I set it down, she became extremely agitated and shrieked something like "you didn't just set that on the ground!" as if it were the American flag or something. I told her as much, and she explained the tube would get "debris" on it. Not "junk," or "dirt," but "debris." While I see the logic in what she was saying, that "debris" can be abrasive to the tube, it became evident that Jeanne had taken a tire changing class somewhere and the instructor said something like "to avoid getting debris on the tube, do not place it on the ground." I don't know why, *but I just found it hysterical that Jeanne would call the crud on the ground "debris." But I digress...*

Just a tad concerned that we now had only one spare tube between the two of us, we took off from her house going north into San Bruno, mostly up El Camino Real. All the while, Jeanne was giving me the tour of her old stomping grounds, pointing out such historic landmarks as the spot where she smoked her first cigarette, and the empty parking lot which used to be a Fotomat where she was "trained." We then headed up Sneath Lane.

I guess I'm getting to be a stronger rider, because my first reaction to the uphill view was that I couldn't make it, and I told Jeanne I probably wouldn't. I'm sure I was near my 2.9 mph bottom speed as I made it up the hill, but I don't know that because my cycle computer died. I have a theory that as long as you don't go under 2.9 mph uphill, you won't fall over.

At the top of Sneath, we saw a little long-haired Chihuahua darting in and out of traffic. I called the little dog over, scooped her up and she kissed me. Now worried my own dog, Maddie, would know I was cheating on her, we began looking for the owner.

Rather than leave the dog with no tags on the street, I told Jeanne I was going to take the dog with me if we didn't find her home, and I would return and try to find the owner later. Jeanne told me I couldn't take the dog home, but she doesn't know that in my time, I've brought home more than a couple of dogs, a couple of horses, a tarantula, a cow, and regrettably, one cat. After a few minutes, we saw a guy looking for something, and it turned out to be his dog. When the dog first saw him, she growled, so it was with great reluctance that I returned her, and we were on our way. I don't know where the heck we went after that so I'll quote Jeanne here:

We went down Skyline to the upper trail along the reservoir, where we stopped to have a snack. We rolled through upper Millbrae, into Burlingame, where we went up just the final block of the infamous Trousdale Blvd. Whew! Going along Skyline Blvd again, it was just so beautiful, but we had gotten a later start because of the flat, and looking for the dog's owner had put us behind a little, so we went along the golf course on down to the bottom opening of Sawyer Camp Trail, where we turned down the hill at Crystal Springs to head back to my place. Flying down the hill felt really good until I heard an odd noise.

I heard the odd noise too. Jeanne had run over something that was pretty big, and she had a flat. The tire had a gash in it. Apparently a huge piece of "debris" had penetrated it. We changed the tire, being careful to avoid getting any further "debris" on the tube. As I was pumping it up, the new tube broke where the valve stem meets the tube...that was our last spare! Jeanne was smart enough to keep the old tube with her, and so she patched that one, and again being careful to avoid getting any "debris" on the tube, I replaced it, pumped up the tube, and then this valve stem broke as well.

All this time we were sitting there, dozens of riders were zooming by asking if we had everything we needed (very nice) and we kept thanking them and telling them we were fine. Then, when we didn't have a tube, nobody came by. Jeanne called her sister, who would have to drive up to our location in her car, pick up Jeanne's keys, drive back home, and then come back with Jeanne's truck.

Finally, while we were waiting for her, a rider came by and asked if we needed help. He reluctantly accepted five bucks for a tube though I'm sure he would have given it to us. I changed the tire, Jeanne's sister arrived and Jeanne sent her home.

As the hole in the tire was big, maybe 3/8 of an inch, to prevent the tube from pushing through the tire, we "booted" the tire with a Balance Bar wrapper. We placed the wrapper on the inside of the tire covering the hole, put the new tube in, again being very careful to avoid getting any "debris" on it, and made our way back to Jeanne's place.

It was a great ride and I definitely want to do it again with a cycle computer and no flats...Jeanne approximates it at 25 miles, but I (as I always do) think it was farther. Best of all, my dog Maddie never suspected a thing!

So Sunday's ride from the Presidio to Fairfax started off with a bang...literally. I had put a set of race tires on Jeanne's bike the night before, and while I can generally put Jeanne away on a hill, she was right on my tail (and what a fine tail it is....) going up to the Golden Gate Bridge. The Bridge was exceptionally beautiful. The fog was lifting, now drifting only under the bridge, and the foghorns were blaring. As we were making our way across the bridge I heard a loud bang. Maybe I need to change neighborhoods, because I thought someone had taken a shot at us, but it was only a blowout on Jeanne's tire. Could I have somehow allowed "debris" to get on the tube, thus causing the blowout?

There was no damage to the tire, and I began changing the tube, of course being extremely careful not to allow any "debris" to get on the tube as the other 90 plus riders on the training ride zoomed by us. Two ALC Training Ride Leader sweeps, Ben and Joseph, stopped for us.

Sweeps ride the back of the pack to insure all the riders finish safely. They either ride with, or behind the slowest rider. Over the course of my training, I've spent a good deal of time with several of them. I have yet to meet one who wasn't incredibly encouraging, caring, and helpful.

Jeanne asked Joseph and Ben if the tire was okay, because apparently my inspection wasn't good enough, and I guess Jeanne's in training to be a wife or something. At this point I knew Jeanne was thinking that it would be better if I just rode along so these two hot young guys could help her, and God forbid they might think she and I were "together." However, at this point, I had changed the first tire yesterday morning, the second, third, and fourth when the two valve stems broke yesterday afternoon, I did two tire changes putting the new tires on for her last night, and now this was the seventh! I wasn't about to give her the pleasure of leaving her alone with these guys.

So I put the tire on and (you guessed it) the valve stem broke. So, once again, being very, VERY careful not to let any "debris" on the stupid tube, I changed the eighth tire. One of the ride leaders suggested my pump might be breaking the stems. The other suggested I hold the valve stems while pumping. So using Jeanne's pump, and carefully holding the valve stem, I pumped the tube almost full and off we rode to Mike's Bike's in Sausalito.

Once there, Jeanne asked one of their employees if the tire was okay and he said it was fine (as I and the two ride leaders had previously told her) and the tube just needed more air. We pumped the tube and, yet again, the valve stem broke. The guy from Mike's Bikes said the tubes I had purchased at Performance were cheap, and weak at the valve stem.

I bought new tubes from Mike's, and now being really, Really, REALLY careful not to allow any damned "debris" on the ninth freaking tube, I changed the tire. Jeanne asked if I would have the other guy at Mike's Bikes inspect the tire before we went, because apparently I didn't look annoyed enough already. He said the tire was fine, just as the two ride leaders, the first employee from Mike's, and I had said. And so, Jeanne satisfied, we were off once again.

The rest of the ride was flat free. Just before we hit Camino Alto we caught up to fellow riders who had also had tire problems. Camino Alto is difficult, but beautiful. Going up we came upon a gorgeous St. Bernard on the road, but I heard someone calling for "Heidi" and I knew she was their dog. Good thing too, because Jeanne was worried I was going to try to scoop the dog up and take her home with me.

I was thinking Jeanne must have eaten her Wheaties that morning or something, because I just couldn't keep up with her on the hills, and this has never happened. Maybe I was just tired from changing all those tires, but eventually, in all the twists and turns, I lost sight of her. At the peak of Camino Alto there is a fork, and right where I would have been waiting for Jeanne had I been in front, there were many other riders, perhaps waiting for their "friends," but no Jeanne. I guessed that I had a fifty/fifty chance of getting it right, and zoomed down the hill on the left fork. It was an awesome downhill, and it would have been perfect had I not been worried that I might have to go back up this hill because I had chosen the wrong fork. Eventually I passed Stephanie, the TRL, and I knew I was headed in the right direction.

We rode on to Fairfax without incident in a group of five now. We had lunch (what I'd call a snack but these guys call it lunch), Jeanne got a compliment on her tires (they're blue) and we were back on the road. The entire way back, and particularly on every hill, I had difficulty keeping up with Jeanne, and we could only determine that these race tires had made her that much faster. I was anxious to try them, and Jeanne was anxious to get rid of them, because (can you believe this?) the blue color doesn't look good with her silver bike "Misty" or "Mystic" or whatever the hell she calls it. If I had a tire that made me that much faster I wouldn't care if it made flatulent noises, forget the color!

Eventually we made it back to the Sports Basement, and for the first time Jeanne made it up the Sausalito Hill without stopping (she did touch her foot down but you couldn't call it stopping). I had a really good weekend of riding, and for the first time in a long while, I rode until I was sore. I'm beginning to think there is a possibility, remote that it is, that I will complete this ride.

Total miles thus far in my training: 2,529

Upon rereading this journal entry, my first inclination was to summarize by saying simply, "Wow! Jeanne's a bitch." When I bounced the idea off Jeanne, she was okay with it, but I finally came to the conclusion others might not "get it." I was concerned some folks would take offense, and think either I really believe she's a bitch, or Jeanne is just, in fact, a bitch. I was troubled others might not understand the friendly antagonism we often share.

When Shelly read this entry she called me immediately and, after saying "Dude! You're fuckin' hilarious!" She said "Why can't that broad change her own flats?!" By the way, thank you for waking me out of a good sleep at 11:45 PM, Shelly. It was well worth it to hear that flowery compliment.

Truth be told, I'm the type of person who loves to do things for people and then bitch about it later. Jeanne is quite capable of changing her own flat. I do it because we're always in a hurry, and I'm much faster than she is. Besides, if I didn't do it, I wouldn't have anything to bitch about.

And what about the constant nagging and concern with debris? What about the second guessing of my work, and the need to have it rechecked not once, not twice, but four times?

Wow! Jeanne's a bitch…

3-20-05 Training Journal Entry

Today's ride was the fifth of a series of ten leading up to the Century (100 Miles) on May first. We rode from the Presidio in SF to Lagunitas, which is a tiny little place nearing Point Reyes. It was a 53-mile ride, and while I have done a few longer rides, this was probably the toughest, with three major hills.

I picked up Jeanne, which is our normal routine now. Jeanne has definitely become my training partner, and we've reached a point where we are comfortable not only riding together, but we have also developed a system of checking each other, and helping each other (you get the food and I'll fill the water bottles).

I was really nervous starting out and I still don't know why. I started very near the front of the group of maybe fifty some riders. Where riders would normally begin passing me at the first hill, we were forced to dismount and walk our bikes due to a scheduled "Fun Run," as there were hundreds, if not thousands, of runners on our path.

While crossing the Golden Gate Bridge, only one rider passed me. We rode on the pedestrian side of the bridge because they had reserved the bicycle side for the runners, and so we had to be extra careful to avoid squishing the tourists.

I held my position in the front ten, and once we crossed the bridge it was all downhill to Sausalito and (heh-heh) then of course, fat guys have the advantage. I passed a couple of our riders going down the hill and after a couple of traffic lights, stopped for a while to let my not-so-fat friends catch up.

We rode into Mike's Bike at a good clip, where we stopped and Stephanie, the cute young Training Ride Leader with the great laugh, decided her tire was low.

While I'm talking about Stephanie, I'm reminded of another rider that, of course, isn't Stephanie, who has the funniest habit. She seems to think if her foot touches the ground, it counts as a stop. So as we all do, she'll call out "Stopping!" But she has mastered the art of barely tapping her toe down. She could be going 35 mph, but as long as that toe touches...it's a stop. Apparently the "No Cop No Stop" rule only applies to stop signs though. You have to make an actual "stop" for a red light.

Anyway, Stephanie had Presta Valves on her tires, and everybody's pumps were set up for Schrader valves. That might be reversed as I never get them straight, but I have a 50/50 chance of being correct. So Alan, Jeanne, and I fiddled with the pumps, and her valves, and all that stuff. By the time we got done Ben, the TRL and sweep for the day, had joined us, and everybody else had gone on ahead of us.

This brings me to my point for the day. I've decided Jeanne and I aren't really that slow, it's just we have RADD (Rider Attention Deficit Disorder). We stop at every excuse for a stop. Stephanie really didn't need us, but we had fun stopping and socializing with her and Alan.

So we finally started back up, and that's when we met Karen "C" ass. Karen was in front of me going up Camino Alto, and I stayed right on her tail (and what a fine...). Okay, look...I'll admit it...when you ride behind someone uphill at 6.5 mph, pretty much your view is their ass.

To understand the name "Karen 'C' ass," you have to know that Cannondale is a company that makes bikes and bike apparel, and they put a "C" logo on the butt cheek of their shorts, and bibs, and tights, which I had only learned yesterday.

Yesterday, Jeanne and I got rained out of our planned ride, and her back up plan was to go work out at her gym. My thinking, however, was if God had intended us to work out, he'd have given us better weather, so we might as well go bike stuff shopping.

While we were browsing through the Supergo bike stuff store, I found some very reasonably priced Cannondale bibs and tried them on over my tights (the previous sentence is one I would never have believed I would EVER in a million years write).

While I was checking them out Jeanne told me I had a "C" on my butt, and I looked and didn't see it, so I asked "Where?" At this, Jeanne pointed and actually touched my "C" to show me where. Of course I, not being one to pass up an opportunity, had to pretend I was completely appalled by her action and made a huge fuss over it.

While riding up Camino Alto behind her, I had plenty of time to notice Karen was wearing Cannondale shorts. So I called out to Jeanne "Hey! Don't touch that 'C!' It's not my butt!" Trust me, there was no chance Jeanne would mistake our butts, and even less chance Jeanne would touch either one of our butts, but I thought it might be good for a chuckle.

At the top of the hill, a fellow rider and TRL, Clay, had broken a spoke, and we all discussed whether he should continue on with a wobbly wheel or turn back to Mike's Bikes for a repair. Stephanie stopped because she's a Ride Leader, Alan stopped because he's a Ride Leader too, Jeanne and I stopped because we have RADD, and Karen stopped because as we were all making "C" butt jokes together, she was officially one of us.

So eventually we were off again and somehow I ended up in front of Karen, who asked if the "C" looked as cute on her butt as it did on mine. I told her she was too young for me to notice. I seldom get butt compliments, so I'm documenting them all (okay, both) in this journal.

Stephanie and I had some fun racing down Camino Alto, but she's a brave young lass and she kicked my tail (and what a fine...) even though she didn't even know we were racing. I learned something new today. When racing down a hill, and leaning into a turn, always keep your inside pedal up. If you don't, and you lean deep enough, your pedal will hit the pavement and you will (literally) bounce. I didn't quite crash, but I did bounce, and nobody wants to bounce on a bicycle at 35 mph, least of all me.

We hit Fairfax in no time, made a brief pit stop and got back on our bikes. We all turned to our fearless leader Stephanie, and it soon became quite apparent she had absolutely no idea where the hell we were going. She stopped, so we all stopped. She whipped out her trusty map, got her bearings, and we were quickly off again! Stephanie made a quick right turn and we all followed. Then a middle-aged lady standing at the corner, who had absolutely no relationship with us, shook her head "No" and pointed to the left. I guessed she had seen other riders going in that direction, and she was trying to get us back on the right path.

Of course those other riders could have been going anywhere and weren't necessarily with our group. We were all forced to make a decision. We could either show our loyalty to our fearless leader Stephanie, who had been trained extensively *to lead us, or we could make a decision based on the head and hand gestures of a complete stranger.*

As we all hung the "U" turn we thanked the lady, and waved "goodbye." Stephanie came with us.

After some time we came to another intersection, and once again Stephanie pulled out her map. She made her decision on the turn, and then a sudden gust of wind caught her map, and we all watched it fly away. Stephanie really knows how to instill confidence!

Apparently, she had no need of the map after that, because before I knew it, we were heading up White's Hill. I have no idea who White is, or why he put that hill there, but he was obviously an evil genius. It is a hard hill, but I've done worse, and I was able to keep the sizzling pace of 4.5 mph up the entire climb. I waited at the top for my chums, but after a bit my legs were getting cold so I rode on with Stephanie.

After that it was an easy five or so miles to Lagunitas. On the way we passed some wild turkeys and so I yelled out "Wild Turkeys." I teased Stephanie, saying I knew she was a drinking woman, because when I yelled "Wild Turkey" her eyes glazed over and she started drooling.

The turkeys were magnificent, and the one male was really strutting his stuff, spreading his tail feathers (and what a fine tail it was) in an impressive display. I once again thought of all the things I might never have seen, had I not signed up for this ride.

So Stephanie and I zoomed along with Karen "C" ass behind us. We were into some serious riding concentration when we heard a bunch of yelling from our right, and now slightly behind us. We had just passed our final destination, the Yellow Door Café in Lagunitas. We hung another "U" and joined the group for lunch.

Jeanne caught up before long, and we ordered. I filled all of our water bottles while Jeanne handled the ordering and the money so we could make a quick get away when it was time to leave. I can't see anything without my reading glasses, so I asked Jeanne if they had something like a mushroom burger. Jeanne suggested the Portobello mushroom burger and then I was off filling water bottles.

So, after way too long (and I'm not blaming the restaurant here as fifty some of us came in all at once) my food came. Okay (I thought)...joke's over...where was the freaking burger?! The only thing on the bun was this huge mushroom. I like mushrooms all right, but on a burger or steak...not as the burger. Sheesh! It dawns on me that on all these rides, not once have we stopped at a single McDonalds, or Burger King, or even a Subway! We keep stopping at these places with fruit cups, and teeny tiny éclairs, and these overgrown radioactive mushrooms where a burger should be! Hey, if the éclairs at the place in Tiburon were as big as this mushroom, I'd be a happy guy! Oh yeah, and a special "thank you" to Jeanne for that great Portobello recommendation. I'm actually writing this journal two days later, and I still can't get that taste out of my mouth.

Pretty much anything is good when you're hungry. Jeanne's food must have been awesome, because she had to wait about a half hour (or more) longer than I. They had apparently given her order to someone else. So really, this time (and this one time only) we were delayed through no fault of our own. We started off together with Karen and Jane, and Jane pulled over almost immediately with a flat tire. She urged us to go on. It was a good thing she did too, or Jeanne and I might possibly still be on the road.

Riding through Fairfax, we stopped where some kids were selling Juice and Vanilla Wafers for fifty cents. I figure any kid ambitious enough to hustle a buck deserves my support. Besides, it was another excuse to stop. Big spender that I am, I treated the ladies to what amounted to about a quarter of a small Dixie cup full of juice and one Vanilla Wafer. I tipped them fifty cents and figured these children must attend the same school as the guy who makes the teeny tiny éclairs in Tiburon.

The kids also had a petting zoo with at least one snake and a large lizard of some sort. We passed on the petting zoo, even if it would have been one more reason to stay off our bikes. We also questioned the little girl who handed us the Vanilla wafers about her physical contact with the reptiles, and her hand washing habits. We'll know the real truth if anyone gets salmonella poisoning.

White's Hill had been an easy ride this direction, but we stopped once more before we tackled Camino Alto. I don't know if it was just because of the rest we took before, but it wasn't all that bad. At the peak of the hill, Alan was waiting for us and cheered us over. He may be canonized someday, and I'm not just talking about getting a "C" on his butt.

We stopped on the way back at Mike's Bikes and bought some Gu for that extra burst of energy to get us over the Sausalito Hill. When we came out of the store it was pouring rain. We waited out the storm a bit, and finally figured it might get worse instead of better, so we should probably get going. The rain did let up a bit and we jumped at the chance. Even still, Jeanne's bike ahead of me was letting up a huge rooster tail of water, and my shoes and pants were getting soaked.

By the time we hit TLFH, it had stopped raining completely. Somehow we bumped into Karen again, and the three of us rode in together. About a half mile from the Sports Basement where our ride would end, Karen zoomed by me and said something like "you better get that C ass in gear." I took that as a *challenge, and the race was on. After 52.5 miles we were racing at maybe 27 mph on a flat. Do I even have to tell you she beat me?*

I thought Jeanne was coming in last so I raced around the corner, jumped off my bike and cheered her in, as if I'd been waiting for her for hours. As it turned out, there was one last rider behind her, and we all cheered wildly for him!

I was very happy that after 53 miles I still had some energy in reserve. All in all it was another fun ride, and my best run up the Sausalito Hill. Despite my earlier misgivings, I really didn't have anything to be nervous about.

2,663 miles thus far in my training

A funny thing happened on the way to Lagunitas. On the way out through Sausalito, I had ridden well ahead of Jeanne, as I almost always do on a downhill. I pulled up at a traffic light next to a fellow ALCer. Across the street we saw a rider who had been pulled over by a police officer, apparently for running a red light.

I told my fellow rider I had once been pulled over on my bike. "For running a red light?" he asked. I told him it was actually for speeding, not having time to get into the rest of the story and explain it was in a regional park where the speed limit was only 15 mph.

He looked at me with the greatest admiration and gave me what I thought was a terrific compliment. He said, "That is so much more butch than getting pulled over for running a red light!" I believe that this is the first time in my life that I, or any of my actions, were described as "butch."

3-26-05 Training Journal Entry my place to Jeanne's place, back to my place, with SFO thrown in.

Jeanne and I were skipping the CAT II Series ride # 6 scheduled for Easter...because it was Easter, and the Easter Bunny had to come and hide eggs and baskets and such, even if my kids are all adults now. Jeanne had family obligations as well. We didn't want to jump from a 53 mile ride to a 68 mile ride because we skipped one week, so we figured something big would be good for Saturday.

Originally we planned to meet in the middle of our two homes, and then ride to Jeanne's place in San Mateo on the border of Burlingame, ride back to my place in Newark, and then back to Jeanne's. Jeanne would then drive us both back to my place to dye Easter Eggs with my family.

Jeanne figured it was 22 miles between our homes, a really bad guess, which probably has something to do with being told "this is eight inches" at some point in her life by some liar. At any rate we thought three trips would be sixty-six miles, which seemed like a good number to both of us.

So we synchronized our watches (not really, but we called each other) and I left my place at 8:00. I took my usual ride to, and then over the Dumbarton Bridge, and down the bike path on the other side of the Bay to Haven Street. From there I rode to Old Bayshore. As Haven Street is the eleven-mile mark, I began scanning the horizon for Jeanne. At the end of Old Bayshore, I was in uncharted territory, and having no idea where she might be now, I called her on her TOP SECRET cell phone number.

For some reason Jeanne has been very reluctant to give me this number...which by the way is 767-3751. She says her cell phone number is for work and emergencies only, and so I should never call it. I'm beginning to think she has another riding companion and she doesn't want him/her to find out about me.

Jeanne directed me to take Woodside Road to Veteran's Blvd. It gets kind of confusing there, so I turned on what was clearly marked "Veteran's Blvd." The first street sign said "Broadway" but I figured it would turn into "Veteran's" any time. A mile later, the street sign names hadn't magically changed, so I went back to Woodside to figure the whole thing out, and there I found Veteran's Blvd. I just missed it the first time.

So about a mile down Veteran's Blvd., Jeanne called me and told me where to go next, left on Whipple, and right on Industrial. It was like having GPS, but more personal. Eventually we met about where the old Circle Star Theater used to be. We checked our mileage, and both of us had ridden 16 miles and some change. At this point I really had to go to the bathroom, so Jeanne thought it would be a good idea to take me on a tour of every fountain on that side of the Bay. Maybe not, but it certainly seemed that way.

We went into Downtown San Carlos, where Jeanne called her sister to see if we could use her bathroom. She wasn't home, which was just as well, because that's not really how I like to be introduced to people ("Pleased to meet you, where's your bathroom?"). Finally we found a Starbucks, I snuck into their bathroom, and then we headed for a bakery called Vivaldi's. They had ham and egg croissants and Peet's coffee. I give them 5 stars...it was great!

We then headed back out to the Bay Trail, which at times heads directly to my house, even though we were going to Jeanne's. So while it was a beautiful ride, it wasn't very direct.

Eventually we made it to Jeanne's place where I sat on her couch and waited while she powdered her nose and such. It must *have been a little while, because I was kind of nodding off. Then she asked if I was ready to go as she passed into the kitchen, which is a sure sign we're leaving soon. I got up...and then I fell down. My legs were completely numb. I tried to get up a few times, but to no avail. So there I was sprawling and flailing around her living room floor like a giant fat squid in spandex.*

Before too long the feeling returned to my legs and I got up like nothing happened, but you know how it is when you're embarrassed even though no one is looking. I did explain it to Jeanne, as I was a tad concerned. Really though, between the elastic on my leg warmers, the elastic on my shorts, and my knees being elevated higher than my butt on her futon, it all made sense (a lot more sense than that last sentence if you read it out of context).

We left and headed back for the Bay Trail. There had been some talk of going to SFO, and I thought it would be cool, if for no other reason than to say I rode from my house to SFO. Besides, Laurie had bought a snazzy new camera for me that will take movies with sound, and I thought it would be cool to take a movie of a jet taking off, don't ask me why.

I'm glad we went that way though, because some of the nicest stuff to see was on this leg of the ride. They have a very rustic Marina over there (who knew) and a lot of great trails with a terrific view of the city. Once we got as close to the airport as the trails would allow, I took a movie of a couple of jets, but the really big one I wanted to get, waited to take off until after I had used all of the memory in my camera.

So we started the long journey to my place from SFO. Jeanne took the lead, and she was keeping a good clip at seventeen plus mph. We went a few miles like this, and then I found myself getting a side ache, which I don't think has happened since I was a little kid running, and got out of breath.

Humiliated, I had to ask Jeanne to slow down, which she graciously did without calling me a wuss.

We rode on for maybe a mile or two more like this, but I finally had to ask to stop completely for a rest. I don't think either of us has ever had to do this before. Still, Jeanne didn't call me any names some folks might associate with a cat. She was as kind and caring as could be.

I was glad I hadn't called her any cat names last week when she had a bad week, and I had only thought them really loud. After a few minutes, I felt much better and we were off again. We rode to a Carl's Jr. in Redwood City, ate some dunch (dinner/lunch), and then we were off to my house...but something didn't feel quite right. We crossed the bridge and rode by the salt ponds. Jeanne refers to these as "a very shallow part of the Bay." She seemed excited the Bay was "right there" as we were riding along. I was just too tired to pay attention, or too lazy to explain right then. At any rate, why ruin it for her?

About two miles from my house, I figured out what hadn't felt right since we left Carl's. I had left my gloves. I did think (very briefly) about turning around to go back and get them, but we were so close. I looked down at my cycle computer and I realized we were averaging just under 14 mph for the ride, so I tried to push it to raise the average over the 14 mark. For me this is generally a good goal.

We didn't make it, but we did average 13.98 mph for 70.5 miles...Not too shabby!

2,757 miles thus far in my training

Jeanne endeared herself to me for life on this ride. In all my years of living, this may have been the strangest event that brought me to the realization that I had a true friend.

I really needed to stop at one point. I'm pretty aware of my body when I'm exerting myself. If I'm riding hard, sometimes it's my legs that are screaming for me to stop, other times my lungs, and occasionally I hear from my heart. When it talks, I listen. And no, before you even ask, I do not extend this same courtesy to all of my organs. On this particular ride, I was worrying a bit. On the return trip, I was feeling some chest pain, and I asked Jeanne to slow for me, and then finally, I had to ask her to stop. Jeanne didn't hesitate one bit, or act the least bit annoyed. She knew all about my heart problems, and even knew where I stashed my Nitro Glycerin, and how to administer it if the need ever arose.

At this point in time, Jeanne and I had ridden less than 200 miles together, and as folks will do when they are newly acquainted, we were still horribly polite to one another. Then, as much as I hate to admit it, there was the whole man/woman thing that keeps a fellow that much better-mannered.

Upon my request, we pulled over at a bench and Jeanne was concerned and caring. She asked if my heart was hurting, and I explained sometimes it's difficult to determine whether it's really my heart that's hurting, or whether I'm having indigestion. I went on to explain that sometimes if I burp, it relieves the pressure in my chest, and then I know it's not my heart that's really hurting.

Jeanne asked, "Why don't you burp?" I told her I was not going to burp in front of her, as she was a lady. Jeanne replied, "what if I burped in front of you first?" Before I could answer, Jeanne swallowed a mouth full of air, and let out a pretty impressive belch.

If Jeanne were a classless boar that either didn't care about how she appeared, or didn't know any better, this episode in our association wouldn't have meant anything, but my friend Jeanne is as ladylike and refined as any woman and I know she was as uncomfortable as hell belching in front of me like that. She did it to keep me from being embarrassed, and that was a pretty sweet sacrifice.

My kids call her "Auntie Jeanne" and I sincerely hope someday I'll have grandkids that call her "Great Auntie Jeanne" or whatever it is kids call their great aunt. The grandkids will ask why she's "Auntie Jeanne" even though she's not Laurie's sister, or mine. I'll tell them this story, and they'll know how the whole thing started with a burp.

Training Ride April 3, 2005 from the Sports Basement

4-3-05 Training Journal Entry

Today's ride was The Nicasio Loop; the seventh in the series of rides building up to the 100 mile mark on 5-1-05. Let me first say I had a bad cold, and a horrible workout week combined with a very physically demanding work week (I'm just full of excuses).

Jeanne and I were running just a tad behind, but we made it in time for the pre-ride stretch and of course, the safety speech. The Golden Gate Bridge was a bit more windy than usual for this time of the morning, and the sky was horribly threatening. There were 71 official riders, and we started mid-pack from the Sports Basement in San Francisco.

At this point, I'm going to have to talk about "last place." One of the ALC mantras is "It's a ride, not a race." We newbies hear that from veteran riders all the time. It's usually the faster riders that say it, trying to make us slower guys feel better. Once, when I was barely inching up a hill somebody tried to encourage me with the "ride not race" speech. Crawling along at 2.9 mph, I said "For God's Sake! Why didn't someone tell me months ago? Here I've been racing all this time!"

Yes it is a ride, not a race, and I'm proud to be riding amongst all these wonderful people, in any position. I'm proud I'm even attempting this ride. That being said, NOBODY WANTS TO BE LAST!

I had a theory that if Jeanne and I simply refrained from our usual social activities with everyone else, we would be in the latter third of the pack, but not last, or second and third from last. We tested that theory this week.

Remember now, our training rides are in the seventy mile neighborhood with steep difficult climbs. There are no wimpy riders left. If there ever were any, they've quit by now. Finishing anywhere ahead of dead last has become a challenging goal for me. Ben and Joseph were the sweeps this week. Ben and Joseph are good, funny, kind, warm guys, and I hoped not to see their friendly faces (except possibly at lunch and breaks). Jeanne was with me on the new "no dilly-dallying" policy, and so we booked. Without so much as a glance, we passed our normal first rest stop, Mike's Bikes in Sausalito.

I think nearly all the remaining riders passed me on Camino Alto, but maybe not. I never saw Ben or Joseph. We picked up Michael (last rides new friend and a fellow former last place finisher) near Fairfax. When we came to "Shady Lane" I knew right where to turn. It's a name that has sentimental family meaning. After Camino Alto, the right on Shady Lane is the only turn I would know to make on my own.

Honestly, I have a horrible sense of direction, and so I generally figure I might as well let Jeanne do all of the navigating. We laugh all the time about my being directionally challenged.

I made the turn on Shady Lane and Michael said something like, "Wow! You really know your way around this place!" To which I coolly replied "Like the back of my hand." Then Jeanne piped in, "Cause when you think of orienteering, you think of Russ!" I laughed so hard I almost fell off my bike.

We rode into Fairfax, and at our normal coffee stop there, I made a quick dash in to refill water bottles, while Jeanne downed a couple of Ibuprofen. We had finally caught up, and if we left now, there were at least twenty people in line for the bathroom who we could get a jump on. We did a "Gu" shot and we were off once again. Jeanne was faster than I, and she was pushing me the whole time. My stuffy nose wasn't helping any, but I was managing. Until this week, I could put her away on White's Hill, which really is a monster. She passed me with little difficulty this week, but I kept within one hundred feet or so of her. She hit the peak, and glanced back to make sure I was okay. I shouted a congratulatory phrase indicating she (for today) was the stronger (rider) of the two of us. Okay, what I shouted was "I'm your bitch!" The phrase comes from a longer, even less politically correct statement "He (or she) beat me up (the hill) like I was his (or her) bitch." Anyway, in some sick way, it was congratulatory.

So for maybe fifteen minutes now I had been pounding away at this hill, pumping rhythmically, my breathing becoming harder, faster, and heavier. I climbed ever closer to the peak, anxiously awaiting the bliss of the downhill, pushing more, and just as I reached the summit I felt almost woozy...no wobbly. I thought I had broken yet another spoke, but it was just a flat tire.

I pulled to the side, whipped out my tire irons and spare tube, and began frantically changing the tube. Before long, the other riders began catching up, and greeted me with "Are you okay?" and "Need anything?" It wasn't just one of them that asked, or a few of them, but every single one of my fellow

76

riders asked if I needed help and it warmed my heart to be a part of this group. I asked Ride Leader, Bob Katz, to ride ahead and let Jeanne know what had happened.

After a while all that kindness gets to be a pain in the ass, because you have to take time out from fixing your tire to answer everybody, and tell them you're fine. Karen "C" ass pulled over with me to act as my "thumbs up'" and keep me company. When we're pulled over, we're trained to either give a thumb up (it's all good), a thumb down (I need help), or cross your wrist in an "X" (it's an emergency).

All too soon they appeared! The dreaded faces of doom, Ben and Joseph, the ever looming sweeps pulled up smiling. Ben joked he and Joseph now had a running bet as to how many miles out they would be before they would run into either Jeanne or I having some kind of mechanical difficulty. Yeah guys...yuck it up! Really, I laughed. I urged Karen to go ahead as her legs were getting cold and that can lead to problems on a ride. Beside, Ben and Joseph were with me.

Before too long I was rolling, and as I knew she would be, Jeanne was waiting for me at the bottom of the hill. That's a buddy! I know she was as disappointed to see Joseph and Ben as I was, but she didn't make a fuss like I would have. It was my fault that once again, we were in last place.

Jeanne started out in front of our pack of four and I just couldn't keep up with her, but Ben and Joseph were good company and they made the trip pretty enjoyable. I don't think I ever lost visual contact with Jeanne, but she was well ahead. We hit Nicasio, which was a scheduled rest stop. There were maybe 20 to 25 riders hanging around and drinking coffee and such.

My bike had been squeaking like a umm...well, like a bike that needed some oil somewhere, so I oiled it everywhere from which I thought it could possibly squeak. Then I oiled a chain for a fellow rider, Nicole, who had complained about her chain squeaking. Within five minutes, and without a snack or drink refill, Jeanne and I were off and far ahead of the pack.

Finally, at one intersection, Jeanne said we had to eat something because lunch was more than an hour away. She pulled some kind of Clif bar out of her bag, and while she was doing it, I could see the pack following us in the distance. By the time we wolfed down our bars, they were approaching. I was reminded of Butch and Sundance looking back at the unknown posse and saying, "Who are those guys?"

We started off, but they had caught us, and some of them passed us at the first intersection. At this turn we were riding straight into a hellacious headwind. A few of us traded off riding in front and breaking the wind, but it was slow and difficult. We finally made it to Samuel P. Taylor Park.

There is a bike path which runs the length of the park. It is completely sheltered from the wind and is lined with huge redwoods and ferns which form an incredible canopy. At many points you can't even see the sky. The ride to this point was worth this little piece of heaven, and if you ever get the chance to visit this park, it will certainly be worth the drive.

At the end of the park there was a restroom calling to Jeanne, and I played with my new camera while I waited. I'd love to show you pictures of this park, but I never quite figured out the newfangled contraption.

So now, our last place position secured once again, we rode into Lagunitas for lunch. Everyone else went to the Yellow Door Cafe, so we headed for the deli next door, hoping it would be a bit faster. It was, and we ate quickly, wanting to get out ahead of at least some of the crowd.

We expected to have a bit of a tailwind when we crossed White's Hill this direction, but the weather Gods can be cruel. The wind had shifted and we had headwinds both ways. The closer we got to San Francisco, the worse the winds became.

We were traveling at 10.5 to 11 mph, and I was struggling. I had run out of water by the time we reached Fairfax. People say there's never a cop around when you need one, but the same can be said for little kids with lemonade stands. You just can't rely on them!

We did Gu shots again before Camino Alto. Gu is a sports nutrition gel which offers an immediate, long-lasting source of energy. At least that's what they'd like us to believe and so they say that in their advertisement. I don't know if it's just psychological, but it seems to help.

At least the wind wasn't so bad going up the hill, but once we cleared it, it was awful. In fact, I have to say this was, without question, the most difficult ride of my life. We struggled to Mike's Bikes.

I couldn't keep up with Jeanne, and at this point I didn't even care that I couldn't. She knew I needed water and she would stop and wait for me at Mike's Bike's in Sausalito. I couldn't think of anything worse than riding into this horrible headwind, except possibly doing it wet. The clouds were black and gathering, and we all knew they were going to burst at any moment. I quickly, almost in a panic, refilled my bottles and just as we were starting up again Jeanne's cell phone rang. You remember the secret cell phone number which nobody is allowed to have, the number which only her work and emergency calls can be made to and from.

I thought it was perhaps the President calling her for some top-secret mission! Maybe it was her boss calling her to make a life or death decision for the company.

It was Edna, probably wanting to play Brady Bunch Trivial pursuit again or something. So now I was in a panic, terrified of the coming storm, and Jeanne was chatting with Edna about doing lunch on Tuesday and has Edna found any cute guys for either of them. I'm not even going to get into the concept that I, the guy famous for the sixteen word telephone conversations can't get the secret cell number, but Edna has it. Edna, who is capable of delivering a four hour narrative on what Jan Brady should do with her hair to distinguish herself not only as a Brady, but also as a person, has the number.

By the way the sixteen word phone conversation goes like this: How are you? How's your car running? Wanna talk to your Mom? Okay I Love you. And yes, I am well aware that I ramble on everywhere else, especially when I write. I just don't like to talk on the phone.

So while Jeanne and Edna were discussing the finer points of asses on Filipino men, the rest of the riders passed us, and the sweeps were waiting with me and watching Jeanne talk on the phone. They kept a polite distance from her, so I told them it was her boss who needed her to make a life or death decision for the company. Oh yeah, and we were once again, dead last!

Some time that spring, the conversation ended and we were off once more. We passed a couple of other riders, and for the first time ever, Jeanne beat me up the Sausalito Hill. I believe the riders we passed when we first left Mike's, passed us up during this climb, but really, when the wind blows that strong, you just try to keep your head down, and everything around you is a blur. When we hit the Golden Gate Bridge, we saw other riders, including Karen "C" ass talking and resting.

If I thought the wind was bad before, it was akin to something you'd expect on Mount Everest going over the bridge. The wind is always bad around the towers, but I was shocked when I got to them. The gusts slowed me to the point that I nearly fell over, and Jeanne literally went backwards for a moment, and then caught herself and put her foot down. I don't know how she got around the tower, but she managed.

Going down the path from the bridge I saw Karen gaining on us, and now I was determined not to be last. Jeanne was right with me and we raced to the Sports Basement. On one of the hairpin turns I could see Karen and we were almost face to face. I was bound and determined she wouldn't "beat" me two weeks in a row. It's possible Karen didn't even known the race was on, but in the end, Jeanne and I weren't last, and actually, neither was Karen. A couple of riders came in behind her, and we rowdily cheered for them all!

Jeanne and I may be last next week. If not, I'm almost certain we will be another day, but this week, victory (or at least avoiding dead last) was ours. Oh yeah, and just after we signed out at the Sports Basement it started pouring. Maybe the weather Gods aren't that cruel after all.

2,837 miles thus far in my training

I get it now… I get it, and I'm ashamed of myself for ever having said, "Nobody wants to be last."

Riding 100, 75, or even 50 miles doesn't come easily to me, but for some, it's an unthinkable impossibility. I'd like to recant my words.

I mention my disdain for last place again in my journal, but next year, when I'm riding in the last position, I may be uncomfortable, but I'll be proud!

4-10-05 Training Journal Entry

Today was the eighth of the series leading up to the 100-mile ride on May first. We rode from the Sports Basement at the Presidio in SF to Point Reyes and back, with a couple of loops thrown in for fun...yeah right.

Riding is a strange hobby which involves more intimate personal details than we normally care to share in polite company. At seventy-five plus miles those details become an intricate part of a ride, and so if you're offended by body parts, or bodily functions, now might be a good time to quit reading this journal.

Today's ride was the longest, and the largest. I've heard rumor there were 120 riders. Whatever the number, it was an impressive crowd. Ben led the safety speech, and once I determined Lydia was going to be the sweep, I figured I should introduce myself as Jeanne and I normally spend a good deal of time in the back of the pack. I'm glad we met, because she's a very nice woman, and we never saw her again.

That's right! Uh huh! That's what I'm talkin' 'bout! Jeanne and I rode with the men and athletic women today and we never saw the sweeps, not even when we stopped for lunch!

Jeanne got clipless pedals and cleats the day before, and I got my new racing tires, and I guess that, combined with our new "no dilly-dallying" policy kept us mid-pack all day.

I should probably mention Jeanne and I worked on our bikes and went for a twenty something mile ride the day before, just so she could try out her cleats, and we could get a little work out. When you're clipped into your pedals, it's frightening at first, because you may forget and take your foot out too late at a stop, and then you fall over without being able to put your foot down. It's a horrible feeling (see training journal from 12-12-

04). Everybody tells you before you get them, you will fall once. I wouldn't stoop so low for a chuckle that I'd tell you Jeanne fell twice.

I'm not going to mention that she fell once right in front of my house, which is just great, because now all of my neighbors think I ride with a drunk. After all, they didn't know she had new cleats.

Nor will I tell you about how she fell in front of Subway where I eat lunch everyday, and where my friends and some of my customers hang out.

Everybody just pretends they don't see you. Now I know this is true because my wife, Laurie, and I watched Jeanne fall from the front door, and when I told Jeanne we had seen her fall, Laurie was angry with me, because she wanted to pretend she didn't see anything.

Jeanne tells me she has lovely large multi-colored matching bruises on both butt cheeks. She isn't a very good sport, or I would have been able to include color photos with this journal entry, but she wouldn't even show me, forget taking picture (yes, I finally have a basic understanding of the new camera). Suffice it to say her sister calls her "Baboon Ass."

I'll also spare you the details of the ordeal of getting the pedals on, and how Jeanne broke the pedal trying to adjust it after I told her not to, and how Laurie and I had to go all the way to Mountain View to get a replacement while Jeanne went to a beer fest. Yes, for the sake of brevity, I won't even mention any of those things. Besides, I'm just not the kind of guy to hold a grudge.

So, Sunday on the ride, we left mid-pack, maybe a third back from the front, and we actually passed more folks than passed us going up to the bridge. We flew down into Sausalito and when I stopped to wait for Jeanne, she was only a couple of seconds behind me. I was riding with Nicole, the woman for whom I oiled the chain in Nicasio last week. When Jeanne caught up, Nicole asked if I was her husband. Later I thanked Jeanne for not saying "Blech Ptooey Yech!" because I believe that was the only phrase she didn't use to make absolutely certain Nicole knew we weren't a couple. She did say "Oh my God, No!" I wondered if it was really necessary for her to be sooo adamant?!

Somewhere after Mike's Bikes in Sausalito, a mini-van made a right turn and cut me off. It was everything I could do too keep from running into the side of his van. Later, I was told he flipped us off as he went by. You have to be pretty brave or pretty stupid to flip off a pack of 117 riders when you're turning into a parking lot. From the way he drove, I'm guessing he was dim-witted, and not so gutsy.

I shrugged it off and we did Camino Alto about a half-mile to a mile per hour faster than ever. We're still slow up the hills, and we didn't pass anyone, and lots of folks passed us, but we are improving.

We were riding with people I didn't know, and in fact hadn't ever seen during a ride before. These were really athletic-looking people with hardly any fat on them. We stopped in Fairfax because I kind of had to go to the bathroom. The line was long, out the door, and this pretty young girl got in line behind me. "I can't keep waiting here" she told me. "I'll probably just have to pull to the side of the road and pee. I've done it before."

I asked if maybe she might be sharing a bit too much information with someone whom she'd known for less than thirty seconds. She laughed and we continued to wait for a bit. Soon she left, I guess deciding to go for the roadside option, and shortly after I decided I didn't have to go that badly.

We rode up White's Hill, it was slow, and hard, and I beat Jeanne up (the hill, I didn't punch her or anything in spite of the fact that she doesn't listen), but we were very close together, and we did it very well. I was proud of us.

As we raced down the hill, the wild turkeys were sitting on a fence maybe six feet from the roadside. I should have stopped to take a picture, but when you work so hard to get up a huge hill like that you really cherish your downhill momentum, and you don't want to give it up for a picture of a few birds. If you want to see what they looked like you can Google "wild turkeys" and I'm sure you'll find a picture somewhere. I later told Jeanne I wouldn't stop on a downhill like that, even if I had a heart attack. We decided any traffic planner that put a stop light at the bottom of a hill never rode a bicycle, or if he did, well then there's a special place in hell reserved for him.

On the way down, I hit a new personal speed record on a bicycle, 39.5 mph. I could have kicked myself for not going for an even 40.

After you make the right turn to Nicasio, you hit a hill which normally would be difficult, but not unbearable. The problem is when you hit it, you're already spent from White's Hill, and there just isn't much left. This week I made it up before Jeanne, but again it wasn't like last week where she was so far ahead I could barely see her. On the way down, I broke 40 mph, and then some pick-up was really insistent about passing me, even though the speed limit is only 35. After he passed I followed him and hit 42 mph.

When we got to Nicasio we stopped and ate Clif bars, refilled the water, and I found a lovely "Porto San" porta-potty. Incidentally, Porto San provided the porta-potties for the Woodstock Concert in 1969. Just in case it ever comes up in conversation, you won't have to feel ignorant now. Oh yeah, and when I say "lovely" I really mean "disgustingly gross."

Jeanne and Alan Kwok were discussing the drama at his workplace, and I didn't want to be rude, but even more, I didn't want to be last. I like Alan, and I could listen to him all day, but I got on my bike and began circling him and Jeanne while we continued the discussion. Jeanne, catching the subtle hint, asked rhetorically if I was ready to leave, mounted up, and we rode.

The stretch from Nicasio to the turn to Point Reyes is maybe the most beautiful place on earth outside of Yosemite. Last week it was so windy, we were in "survival" mode, and couldn't really enjoy it. This week the lakes were like mirrors, reflecting the beautiful hills behind them. The riding conditions were perfect, and while last week we were fighting to stay at 10 mph, this week we were clipping along at 15 mph effortlessly.

Once we turned at the purple bridge to Point Reyes, there were some surprise annoying hills. We took them with no problem, and were rewarded with some long-sloping downhills. It was several miles to Point Reyes, and I only recall one rider passing us, and a couple of others resting at Point Reyes, which, by the way is nothing to write home about. Maybe I just didn't check it out enough, or maybe I was flying through too quickly (but I doubt that). Whatever the reason, as much as I've heard of Point Reyes, there wasn't much to it.

After the little town, Jeanne had heard there was a pretty serious hill. I don't know if it was the placement on the route, or if it really was that big, but it seemed like a monster. On a scale of one to ten it was an eight for difficulty and a nine for distance. It seemed larger than White's hill, and definitely longer. We just picked our way through. I kept setting tiny goals, the next spot in the road or the next traffic sign, and I broke it down that way. It seemed like it was only a few weeks and we were done with it.

Next we looked for the turn off to the heavenly trail through Samuel P. Taylor Park. You can either take the wonderfully paved bike trail through the gorgeously scenic park, or, if you miss the turn, you can take what appears to be the road to hell. It is full of potholes and cracks which seem to be made to suck little skinny bike tires in them. The road is narrow and winds enough so there is no way traffic can pass you. Neither is there any place you can go to get out of the way without risking death or permanent injury, and the drivers are sufficiently annoyed at you that they tailgate. You can feel the heat from their radiators like hot breath on the back of your neck. We, of course, missed the turn and therefore, by default, chose the latter path.

We weren't even positive we missed the trail. Let's be honest here. I, as usual, hadn't a clue where the trail was, or even if there was a trail any where around us. I just relied on my guide, Tonto McArthur, and when we reached the far end of the trail, where it meets the road, she was pretty much sure then we had missed it.

The good news was we only had two more miles of this crappy road, and the Yellow Door Cafe and lunch would be just a mile or so beyond that. Eventually we came to a sign which said "Yellow Door Cafe just ahead" or something like that, and we both let out a spontaneous cheer. This had been a long hard ride. As we turned in the lot, my odometer was reading just under 50 miles, with long hard climbs, and all before lunch.

We ate at the deli again to save time, and besides, they make a pretty good sandwich and fruit salad. I also had some Fritos, because when you ride this hard, you can pretty much justify eating anything. Alan the psychologist, who shall be known as Psycho Alan from now on so he won't be confused with Alan Kwok, came in after we were already well into our lunch. Usually we see him, but he's always passing us. I suspect he usually comes in five or ten minutes ahead of us.

After he got his meal he joined us. I think he'd like it if he knew I was calling him Psycho Alan, because he is probably the most serenely mellow person in the world. He was good company. We sat and marveled at all the faces we had never seen before, because we are always in the back of the pack. It was like a whole new world, and Jeanne and I kept commenting on our keeping up with the big guys.

We knew we couldn't lounge too long if we wanted to maintain our position, so far too soon we were back on the bikes. We headed up the easy side of White's Hill, and in the distance we could see the wild turkeys. A bit later, we saw a male and a female getting romantic. I desperately wanted to pull my camera out and make turkey porn, but I suddenly realized I didn't have the energy. I had waited too long to eat, and I think I was in the early phases of "bonking."

I told Jeanne I felt like I didn't have anything left. She felt pretty much the same but said soon our blood sugar level would elevate and we would be fine. I knew she was probably right, but in the interim, I was a bit miserable.

It takes a pretty long ride for me to get butt pain anymore, but I was suffering. I have heard horror stories from people. I have heard of saddle sores which got so bad they required lancing and antibiotics. Women have told me about blisters on their most sensitive of areas (sheesh, they don't hold anything back), and you commonly hear about raw "lady bits." I don't know anything about that, but I know your ass has to be seriously hurting before you try to position yourself on the saddle in such a way that your testicles absorb the impact instead of your tush.

Once you hit the peak of White's Hill, it's pretty much downhill or sloping all the way to Fairfax. We looked for the lemonade kids because Jeanne had brought ALC bracelets for them (they really liked ours), but they weren't there. Just as well, because I didn't want to take the time, and as Jeanne had predicted, I was feeling much better now, though my butt, and now my toe, of all things, were really hurting.

We stopped at our resting spot before the return trip over Camino Alto and did Gu shots. A couple of riders passed who we didn't know, and then Ben, the ride leader who normally sweeps, rode by. We bragged about how we hadn't had any mechanical problem, but we didn't want to jinx it, so we weren't too exuberant. We still had quite a few more miles to go, and two big hills.

We sang Cat Stevens songs over Camino Alto. Jeanne amazes me, because she's too young to know his stuff, but she knows every word and harmony. It made the hill much more enjoyable and within seven or eight songs, half of which I had to quit in the middle because I forgot the lyrics, we were at the peak. The ride to Mike's Bikes went quickly, and Jeanne had to stop to attempt to order a part for her bike rack. With that done, we hit the road and we were soon facing TLFH, the Sausalito Hill.

I remember the first time I did this climb in between my bike Godmother, Shelly Ross, and Julie Brown, and Julie sang "High Hopes" to me while I suffered up the hill. It seemed like such an insurmountable obstacle then. Now it's just something we do every week, and every week it gets more familiar, and a bit easier. You know where you have to push, and where you can let up. I try to look at it as a series of small rests, instead of one big hill. Jeanne did it without much difficulty at all.

We zoomed across the bridge and into the city, and pulled into the Sports Basement ahead of many people. We couldn't pat ourselves on the back enough. We waited and cheered a few riders in. I wanted to stay and cheer them all in, because God only knows when I'll be in a position to do that again. We watched riders come in who I said I had never ridden with, and Jeanne said she'd never even seen them before. These were real athletic people we were riding with, and we amazed ourselves by doing it.

I hope someday to ride with Lydia the sweep, because she really is nice, but we left the Sports Basement without seeing her all day long!

2,941 miles thus far in my training

It was on one of these rides along in here that Karen "C" ass told Jeanne and I she was riding with three or four of her friends, but I never saw the whole group together until lunch. As it happens, one of her friends was Jeff, the red-haired fellow I signed up with on October 17th. I was glad to see he was persevering in his training. We all said a very quick "Hi" at the Yellow Door Café in Lagunitas, at lunch.

After the ride was over, back at the Sports Basement where we were less rushed, Karen introduced me to "her friend," Jeff. I said something about it being a small world, and that Jeff and I met when we signed up. I asked how long they had been friends, and Karen answered they had met this morning.

She asked how long Jeff and I had known one another, and Jeff replied tongue-in-cheek, "we met in October…We go way back!"

That's how it is when you're riding, though I haven't yet figured out why. "Friendships" form at light speed, when in reality, you might not know a thing about your "friend" except they ride at your speed, and you can count on them if you need them.

It always shocks me when I see fellow riders in their street clothes. I remember one day I was going to pick Shelly up to drive her to the ALC kick off party. She said she'd be waiting in front of her building for me. When I got there I was a little miffed, because as I glanced around, there was no Shelly, just some good-looking woman leaning against the wall waiting for someone. She was practically opening the car door before I realized it was Shelly.

April 18, 2005 Training Journal Entry - The Cheese Factory

This was the ninth ride in the series. I had heard of the Cheese Factory on my very first ride, and so I was curious as to what it would be like.

We started off the day with some wonderful banana nut bread which Jeanne made. It was excellent so I won't even make a joke about it.

We made it with no problem for stretching and the safety speech, but Jeanne was uncomfortable with her saddle, a discussion which we won't go into this week, and so I changed it out during stretching. We had all kinds of problem, and I hate working in a panic situation, but eventually we got it done, listened to the safety speech, and we were off.

We started in the front half of the pack, and again this week, we never left it. We did Camino Alto faster than ever, and we even passed someone! Of course tons of people passed us, but for the first time ever, we passed someone else going up Camino Alto!

91

Somewhere before Fairfax, we got into one of those awkward moments with a car in which we couldn't decide who would go first. It looked like she was letting us go, and then kind of abruptly went in front of us. Jeanne slammed her brakes without unclipping her shoes, and down she went. As I had been the one who talked her into getting cleats, I felt horribly guilty...yet again. When we got to Fairfax, I tightened Jeanne's cleats on her shoes, and loosened her pedals where the cleats snap in, and then we were quickly back on the road to maintain our position.

The climb up White's Hill went really well for both of us. When we hit the downhill I went first, and I saw Jeanne leave without any problem behind me. I sped down by my wild turkeys on the bottom of the hill, and used the momentum to zoom about another mile when I realized either Jeanne had switched helmets somewhere, or a more likely scenario, the rider in the distance behind me wasn't Jeanne. So I stopped and waited, and it was Nicole who came by and said Jeanne had flatted. I crossed the road, and went part way back up the hill to help her out. Someone had stopped to lend a hand, but as soon as Jeanne saw me, she said something to him and he was gone. Jeanne had started the tire changing process, but she didn't have a spare tube, even though in the Training Ride Calendar Page under "Important Things Cyclists Should Know...What you need to bring...Mandatory Items:" Article four clearly states: Spare tube and or patch kit.

Let me just say I was appalled she would be so neglectful, and she would show such blatant disregard, such utter disdain, for the rules. I gave her my spare, changed her tire and we were off.

I've mentioned before I would love to take a picture of all the turkeys, but I'm always running 35 mph right at that point *and there is no way I'd ever stop. But here I was, and there they were, and though I couldn't get them to pose and smile for me, or capture that special turkey porn moment, I did get a couple of okay pictures I'm pretty happy about. I guess Jeanne's flat was God's way of saying, "stop and take a picture." We rode on beyond Lagunitas, and over the Olema Hill from the reverse direction as last time. We went through Olema and then through Point Reyes, again, the opposite direction we went last week. I'll give a little more credit to the town of Point Reyes, it's prettier coming from this direction, but it still smells bad. We passed all of our fellow ALCers sitting eating lunch on the elevated sidewalk in town. We had decided we would ride on to the Cheese Factory and eat lunch there, making up some time, and it would give us perspective as to how far behind the rest of the pack we were.*

The Cheese Factory Hill is a monster, the likes of which I have never ridden. As far as you can see, it never ends. It climbs into the sky until it fades into the heavens. At least that was my first impression. It is the hardest, steepest, longest hill I have ridden to this point. Slowly, but surely, we climbed to the top. I did consider stopping and resting, but I continued on, just staying over the 2.9 mph, falling over sideways point.

After the summit, it was only a short ride to the Cheese Factory, and it is a really beautiful place to rest and eat lunch. I wasn't thrilled with the sandwich, but the scenery was more than worth the price of the meal. We had a nice time, and our fellow riders were, as always, pretty entertaining.

Far too soon we were getting ready to leave. Jeanne had been having some difficulty with her saddle, and I offered to adjust it for her. She didn't want to take the time so we started off, only to find she had her second flat of the day. We had used my spare earlier, because Jeanne can't be bothered with rules,

93

so we had to borrow a tube from Bob Katz. A pretty young girl, Leah, came to observe and learn how to change a flat. We made quick work of it, and left with Karen "C" ass and "the kid," a very young man we have ridden with a few times now, following. Jeanne and I soon put a chunk of ground between us and the other two riders. The backside of the Cheese Factory Hill was far easier than the front, and before we knew it we were in Nicasio, where it finally became painfully obvious to Jeanne that we needed to do something with her seat.

We stopped to adjust it. While we were paused there, Leah and her friend Rick came by. They asked if I was missing anything...like my pump, which I had left at the Cheese Factory. I laughed, and told them earlier that morning some nice young lady brought my keys to me, which I had left on my bumper. As I started to ride away, everybody pointed out I had left my camera on the sidewalk.

We rode over the backside of White's Hill and then passed Fairfax. We came across some more kids selling lemonade in front of a church. They looked so official there. I thought it was quite clever when I learned they weren't selling lemonade for the church, it was purely a private, for profit enterprise. They were literally pulling in money hand over fist!

We stopped at our regular Gu shot benches before Camino Alto, and this was the smoothest quickest ride over thus far. We were feeling pretty darn proud of ourselves! We made one last quick stop at Mike's Bikes for water and we flew up the Sausalito Hill. Okay, maybe "flew" is an exaggeration. But considering we already had eighty miles and change behind us, we did pretty well.

We rolled into the Sports Basement parking lot victorious. While it was difficult and challenging, this was our best ride thus far, and my finest riding moment!

Oh yeah! I broke the 3,000 mile mark during this ride.

3,052 miles thus far in my training

The wild turkeys just beyond White's Hill

Lydia's Story

There are many stories from the road which people have shared with me, which have either moved me, or given me a chuckle, but this one stands out in a class by itself, not only for it's content, but also for it's delivery. My friend, Lydia Winkeller, shared this with a few of us while we were lunching in Point Reyes during a training ride one day. Lydia truly knows how to spin a yarn!

Lydia is a Marinwood mom. She has four kids, among them a set of four year old twin girls. She's involved in "Mothers of Multiples," heavily involved in her kid's schools, and her license plate, on both her bike and her car is "BIKEMOM." She's almost my age, but looks far younger. She's a tall, pretty blonde, and I have to say, she's always made me think of a television mom.

Quite a few riders were sitting on an elevated curb when a group of young gentlemen walked by, and a look of surprise came over Lydia's face. Lydia called to one of the young gentlemen, "MY CROTCH DOCTOR!" She ran over to the shocked young man. He was a meticulously dressed and groomed Asian gentleman with a horribly stunned look on his face which told me he was definitely NOT her gynecologist. Lydia asked "Don't you remember me?"

Crotch Doctor only responded with a very confused look. With that, Lydia pulled her cycling shorts out and only slightly down, as if to expose her crotch to the young man and jar his memory. "Does this help?" she asked.

Crotch Doctor only appeared to be more confused and bewildered, and just a bit offended. Lydia explained early in the week of one of the previous AIDS/LifeCycles, her "crotch" became so chafed it was bleeding. She went to the medical tent, and they suggested she quit riding, but Lydia wouldn't hear of it. Their solution was to tape Lydia's "crotch."

Crotch Doctor was actually a nurse practitioner who volunteered his time that year as a Roadie in the medical tent, and he drew the assignment of taping Lydia.

There are no buildings in most of the camps on the ride, only tents, and so for Lydia's privacy, the taping procedure took place in the back of a van with tinted, almost mirrored, windows. Lydia said she hopped in the back of the van with crotch doctor, dropped her shorts, and let the taping begin. She said she lay on the floor of the van, legs spread, so the crotch doctor might do his work. Of course, at first she was terribly embarrassed and made some attempt to cover "herself." But as this became a daily routine, by the latter part of the week, she had pretty much just resigned herself to being exposed.

One morning, as Lydia lay in the back of the van baring herself to the Crotch Doctor, a gentleman happened by, and using the windows of the van as a mirror, began combing his hair. Lydia says the hair-comber probably couldn't really see her while he was combing, and he certainly had no idea what was going down (so to speak) in the back of the van. But when Lydia saw his face in the window, she was startled and let out a scream. Crotch Doctor, alarmed by Lydia's shriek, screamed too, and upon hearing all this, Hair-Comber was determined to find out what was happening in that van. He pressed his face against the window cupping his eyes.

Crotch Doctor, in a chivalrous attempt to save Lydia from exposure, used what he had to cover her; his body. So as Lydia describes it, there they all were, her, naked from the waist down, legs spread, Crotch Doctor on top of her, both of them screaming, and Hair-Comber peering into the window watching all this and wondering what the hell was going on. Lydia said she thinks Hair-Comber waited outside, at a safe distance, to make sure she was okay. I think he was waiting for his turn.

Of course we were all rolling at the telling of Lydia's story. All of us, that is, except Crotch Doctor, who could only manage an awkward smile as he quietly said, "Oh yes, I remember you now..." to Lydia.

Crotch Doc and his friends were very nice, and asked if any of us had cards with contact information so they might sponsor us for the ride, and those of us who had them whipped them out quickly. I think one of them sponsored Jeanne. For me though, the story was more than enough.

4-24-05 Training Journal Entry

This was the last of the series of rides leading up to our first official century next week, "Day on The Ride." Today's ride was called "The Cheese Factory and Beyond" but it really did seem like we went to "infinity and beyond."

First off, I'd like to say I'm a bit embarrassed my homepage ran out of room and I had to start a second page for my training ride journal. Sometimes I wish I were one of those journal writers who was really brief:

_____, _____, and I rode to _____. It was _____ miles with some _____ hard hills. It took _____ hours and _____ minutes. I felt great!

Mine would go like this:

Jeanne and I rode to _____. It was _____ miles with some really _____ing hard hills. We were_____ minutes late. Jeanne fell_____ time(s) and had _____flat tire(s).

My wife Laurie and I went out with our daughter Erin, and her beau Larry, the night before to celebrate our 27th anniversary, and I had to be up at 4:15 to get to San Francisco for this ride, so I had about three hours and fifteen minutes sleep to prepare for this major undertaking. Though we had a great time with Larry and Erin, I won't do that again! We were moments late for the safety speech and Ben yelled at us right away "You can't sign in!" So we were both not "officially" on this ride. No worries though, I know these guys now, and they aren't just going to leave us lying on the road somewhere, so we just made jokes about not having to follow the rules.

As soon as we left I felt tired and weak. I hadn't ridden or worked out at all the prior week except for the day before. Saturday I did a 27-mile jaunt with Jeanne around my place, and a 10- mile cruise with Erin in Santa Cruz. Both were lots of fun, but for some reason, those rides were hard on my tush. Today I was wearing my best shorts, and lots of butt butter (it's not as gross as it sounds, it's a lotion-like lubricant you put on your skin and your shorts) to fight off chafing.

I waited for Jeanne at the far end of the Golden Gate. I had gotten pretty far ahead of her, and I decided, since we legally weren't on the ride, we needed to stay close today because we should really only count on each other for help.

We zoomed through Sausalito, but we both had to make a bathroom stop at the soccer fields by the Marsh. We met Shiv there, the woman with the cool hot pink dreads. The guy with whom Shiv was riding asked if I had anything he could use to cut his helmet straps, as they were too long and were slapping him in the wind on the downhills. I replied that of course I did, as I was Mexican, and we all carry knives.

I think he thought I was joking until I reached back to my bike pack and with one motion pulled out my knife and snapped the blade open. The blade was perfectly sharp and went through his straps much easier than I had thought it would. I almost cut the poor guy, as he was still wearing his helmet when I cut the straps. I apologized but he was quite adamant everything was fine, and I'm hoping it wasn't just because I had a knife to his neck...mental note...next time remove helmet before cutting straps. How unbelievably stupid none of us thought of this!

I took a movie going down Camino Alto, and I just couldn't keep Jeanne in the frame as I was trying to ride safely with one hand, steering and braking, and taking movies with the other. Was it only four months ago that I said I couldn't point out obstacles on a downhill if the Pope were lying on the side of the road?

Things were pretty uneventful until we were pulling into Fairfax. Jeanne noticed her back tire was a bit low, as was mine. I added air to my tire, and then when I tried to fill Jeanne's tire, the valve stem broke. Fortunately Jeanne had brought a spare, and also a spare spare, as she planned to return the one she borrowed from Bob Katz last week, and Bob wasn't there anyway.

I replaced the first tube with the broken valve stem, and though I was very careful, I broke the valve stem on the second too. We used her last spare, and now we had one spare between us, with maybe eighty some miles still to go. By the way, I now make it a point to drag the new tube around as much as possible, and Jeanne sighs a lot, but she never actually uses the word "debris" anymore. Jeanne apparently stays up nights putting cuts on her valve stems to exact her revenge. Oh yeah, I also checked her cleats to make sure they were tight, and "loosened" her pedals more because she was having difficulty unclipping.

Between the soccer field bathroom stop, and the flat repairs, Lydia the sweep had caught up to us. I had to make another bathroom stop here, and then we were off. I always tell Lydia I'm hoping not to see her all day, but as I told her later that day, she is the most beautiful woman I have ever tried to avoid.

Apparently White's Hill had grown since last week, because it was much more difficult this week. The hill going into Nicasio, also known as the Nicasio Hill (glad someone finally told me) was difficult for me today as well. In fact I might as well just say it, the only part of the ride that wasn't hard were the downhills.

So we rode through Nicasio without resting, and then made the right on Point Reyes-Petaluma Road and up the God-awful Cheese Factory Hill. We decided not to have lunch at the Cheese Factory, but only to make a quick stop. We had Clif bars and Gu shots, refilled water bottles, and hit the road beyond the Cheese Factory.

Everywhere I have ridden thus far, I've seen some beautiful scenery, but this trip from the Cheese Factory to Point Reyes could compare to any. I'll come back here often, in my car. We were already cold, and we had just discussed how unhealthy it might be to be this cold for this long, and then it rained on us. Fortunately that didn't last long, but enough to make us colder, and now wet.

We had heard stories of the "Marshall Wall." I'm told it is more difficult than anything on the ride. We kept climbing little hills as we approached it, and I kept hoping each hill was it, and the "Marshall Wall" was really an inside cycling joke, kind of like snipe hunting. But when we came to the Marshall Wall, it was definitely no joke.

I'll try to quote Jeanne as best I can. She said something like "I always wondered what it would look like. I wondered if it would be like this gigantic monolith coming out of the ground, and now that I see it, umm...it pretty much is."

What we could see of it was worse than anything we had done, and what we didn't know then was it turned and went up even higher. We rode just above the 2.9 mph mark, and when Jeanne felt she couldn't stay over it anymore, she began walking her bike. I rode the whole way, but Jeanne's walking pace was as fast as my riding.

The hill has two false summits, meaning you think you've made it and when you reach that point, you find there's more hill that wasn't visible until you got there. You ride to the next summit, and the Wall breaks your heart yet again. After a bit, Jeanne got back on her bike, and when we were nearing the final summit, she fell. At this point I was really wishing she would stop falling, because I'm running out of guilt (or so I thought) and jokes about falling.

Jeanne is one of the most beautiful, wonderful people I have ever met. She also has the greatest sense of humor, or I would never write about her as I do. All of my joking is meant in good fun, she takes it just that way, and she can give it back just as well as she takes it. I would never want to do anything to hurt her, and so it troubled me horribly when I made the following discovery.

Jeanne had been unable to unclip her foot from her pedal, and even lying on the ground, she was still attached in a tangled mess. She took off her shoe, still attached to the bike, and then yanked the shoe from the pedal with a burst of adrenaline. I pulled out my little multi-tool to adjust her pedal, and lo and behold, I realized every time I'd "loosened" her pedal thus far, I'd actually been tightening it. My guilt was almost unbearable. I probably just shouldn't have said anything, because the peak of the Marshall Wall is a lonely place to die, and Jeanne had every right to react with violence. She didn't react at all. She could have at least thrown the shoe at me.

After her spill, while Jeanne took a moment to compose herself, Courtney, and then her riding partner Kate, passed us as they nearly always do on the hills. It's a constant game of cat and mouse between them and us. They are strong, fit, athletic, beautiful young women. For some strange reason though, we always manage to pass them on the downhills (hmm...), and I think we are a bit faster on the flats. Also, we are less social than they are, since implementing our no dilly-dally policy.

When we hit the peak, later that spring, we paused to take pictures, and take in the beauty of the world. From this vantage point it appeared everything was downhill from here. I felt like I was on top of the world, and at least very near the top of the food chain. I was on top of the Marshall Wall!

There were a few rolling hills before we hit the town of Marshall. It is such a picturesque little place with small boats anchored throughout the little bay, and rustic cabins along the shoreline. We passed Hog Island Oysters, and the air was filled with the smell of Barbecued oyster. I'm not an oyster kind of guy, but we were starving, and they smelled pretty darn good at that point.

We passed Kate and Court on one of the rolling downhills, and kept maybe a quarter mile ahead of them as we rolled towards Point Reyes. Not long before we got to town we passed a stripped spine of some animal (at least I hope it was an animal) and I think Jeanne called out "Spine!" as you would "Glass!" or "Gravel!"

If we were a little taken aback by the spine, I was aghast as I passed a partially decomposed deer carcass, and I called out "Oh, Deer!" When I say, "partially decomposed," I'm being very polite. It was a horrifically ghastly sight. It had probably been hit by a car, and then ripped up and eaten by some animal. It was almost torn in half, and its little deer feet came just a bit onto the road.

Jeanne passed and gasped, but we handled it maturely. About a quarter mile later we heard a terrified blood-curdling scream from Court and Kate behind us, letting us know they too had seen the deer. It was funny because by now, Jeanne and I

103

were so exhausted, neither of us made the slightest reaction to their shriek.

We arrived at Point Reyes and quickly looked for sustenance. We found a grocery store with a deli in the back. While Jeanne was waiting for our order, I went to the big doors in the back of the store, where all grocery stores have their bathrooms. There were two employees chatting away. I waited for a pause in the conversation and asked if they could please direct me to a restroom. They knew they were standing in front of a bathroom, and they knew I knew they were standing in front of a bathroom, but they directed me to the gas station at the end of the street, and told me I'd need a quarter. I could tell they'd done it a thousand times before.

So before I go on, let me just say, I've spent my last dime in Point Reyes. I vow from here on out, I'll buy my lunch in any of the beautiful, bike-friendly towns, like Fairfax, Nicasio, or Lagunitas. I'll buy my sandwich at the Cheese Factory, but Point Reyes is a ride-through from now on. Besides, the place smells awful.

As if to reinforce my feelings for this little town, as we stopped at a stop sign at the edge of town, with one foot planted on the curb, some dumb ass pulling a boat approaching the size of the Titanic, yelled something out his window at us in a very angry tone. As he turned the corner, I glared at him and cleverly yelled "WHAT?" Now he could see my angry face, and realizing I was Mexican, and probably knowing we all carry knives, he changed his tone as if he were making a polite suggestion. He said, "You guys should keep your bikes off the road. It's a dangerous road you're riding on." I think pretty much any road on which some dumb ass is pulling an illegal oversized load is dangerous for a cyclist.

So, never having found a restroom in Point Reyes, and unwilling to drop a quarter in their pay toilet, we rode on. We detoured a mile or so into the Point Reyes National Park, found a bathroom, and, that done; we got back on the route.

My bike Godmother, Shelly, had been calling on my cell phone since Marshall. She was planning on meeting us, and at least doing part of this ride with us. She called several times, as if she didn't know the "no cell phone rule" on ALC rides. Ahh! But we weren't "officially" on the ride, so I kept her posted as to our location. We met her and her buddy Arthur at the bottom of the Olema Hill. It was great to see her.

The only time we actually rode together was through Samuel P. Taylor Park, because going back up the Olema Hill, the three of them, Shelly, Arthur, and Jeanne, put me away. Sammy P. was as beautiful as I remembered it, and we did find the bike trail, though it was easy to see why we missed it before. Starting from the road it's as if somebody spilled a bit of gravel, and then perhaps 30 feet from the road, the pavement begins.

We had a lot of fun and lively conversation through the park. Once we hit the road again, Shelly, on her new super lightweight bike, Robbie, and Arthur pretty much left us in the dust. For a while they waited for us at the hill tops. We picked up Leah going up the backside of White's Hill. She passed me at the peak as I waited for Jeanne. Then going down I passed her and a lot of traffic.

We ambled through the neighborhoods in Fairfax, and Shelly and Arthur passed us again. Jeanne and I were struggling. In Fairfax, Shelly, Arthur, and now Leah, stopped at the little coffee shop we always hit on the way out of the city. Jeanne and I kept plodding along. Eventually they passed us before we hit Camino Alto, and we never saw them again. We stopped at the Gu shot bench and rested, and did our Gu shots, *as always. Then we took Camino Alto. I felt a bit rejuvenated, and even after these eighty miles, it wasn't so bad.*

At the bottom of the hill, we met Court and Kate, and their friend Kathleen who had just gotten a flat and crashed coming down Camino Alto. She had some pain in her wrist, but she thought she was okay to go on. We, as in Jeanne, gave her some Ibuprofen, and we continued on our way.

By now I needed a bathroom again, and we knew we wouldn't make it to the Sports Basement before they closed, so we agreed to head to Mike's Bikes. They were closed too. Thinking about leaving the Sports Basement well before they opened (and they open early on Sunday for us), and getting back well after they close, made me feel I'd been on my bicycle a very long time. It turned out to be eight hours and thirty-four minutes of rolling time. The computer doesn't count stoplight times or when you're still on the saddle, but not rolling.

We stopped at a public bathroom in Sausalito which Tonto...err...Jeanne had scouted earlier in the day. Then we quickly whipped through town and hit the last hill, up to the Golden Gate. We must be getting better at it, because instead of huffing and puffing, we were able to bitch and moan about each little leg of the climb all the way to the top. It really was a struggle, and there was just absolutely nothing left in the tank, and yet we knew we could do it.

One last time, we passed Kate and Court on the Golden Gate Bridge. I guess they must have passed us while I was in the restroom. Then of course it was all downhill! We couldn't wait to get back in the warm truck, where we would devour every bit of leftover food, and some bagels left for us at the Sports Basement.

My cycle computer is off some, I think about two miles per every hundred, but just before we turned into the Sports

Basement it turned over 100.25 miles for this ride. We have to add about two or three miles for our bathroom detour at Point Reyes, but officially...well let me just quote Lydia here:

95.4 miles. 8293 feet of climbing. That's EIGHT THOUSAND, TWO HUNDRED NINETY THREE FEET! No candy asses here, I tell you! ...Oh, yeah. Did I mention NINETY-FIVE MILES, BABY! NINE BIG CLIMBS! MARSHALL FREAKIN' WALL!!!!!!!!!!!!!!! 8293 feet of climbing. WE ROCK!

We do rock, we certainly do.

3,211 miles thus far in my training

.

Once again, on this ride, I was reminded of the intense and almost rushed familiarity riding together brings. When Jeanne and I stopped to assist Kate, Courtney, and their friend Kathleen at the bottom of Camino Alto, Kathleen was in pain, and her wrist was slightly swollen.

I volunteered that "we" had some Ibuprofen. Even though it was Jeanne's stuff, I knew unequivocally, on the road, what's hers is mine and vice versa. To my way of thinking, it was mine to offer.

One of the twins, as we called them, Kate or Courtney, asked if we'd been friends since childhood, and we both jokingly lied we'd only been riding together since 1980. They believed us, but we finally told them we were only kidding. When they finally asked how long we'd actually been riding together, we took a moment to figure it out.

Though we met briefly on January 22, and rode for a while together on the Punch and Pie ride the next day, we couldn't really say we started riding together until February 12th. It seemed inconceivable we'd only been riding as a team for 71 days, and in that time, we'd done eleven rides together, and covered maybe 600 miles. Shoot, by then we were practically cousins! Honestly, it does seem like we've known each other since childhood.

Maybe our familiarity comes because of the interdependence we share. At every training ride, at the end of every safety speech, they always implored us to watch out for one another, and take care of each other. We riders all took those words to heart, and a very genuine caring had developed between all of us. But I know Jeanne watched after me particularly, and she knew I was there for her as well.

She's mentioned her sisters were happy she was riding with me, and Laurie liked my having a riding partner, just in case anything should happen. In fact, it was about this time Laurie suggested I ask Jeanne if she would be my tentmate.

A few people had broached the tentmate subject with me. Interestingly enough, none of them were men. Jeanne seemed like the obvious choice, but I wasn't sure how she'd feel about it (she wasn't one of those who had asked me). Besides, the whole man/woman thing was awkward anyway, but I still felt it was less uncomfortable than camping with a guy in my tent.

When I approached Jeanne, her first response was to make sure Laurie was fine with the idea, but if Laurie didn't have any concerns, then it was a done deal, and we were officially tentmates-to-be. While I was still not completely at ease, it was one of the biggest worries about the trip for me, and I was glad to have it resolved.

Alan and Shelly, Day on The Ride

May 1 2005...The Big One...Day on The Ride...My first Century

My day started at 3:15 in the blessed AM and I ran around getting my stuff together with my eyes burning like I smoked too many cigarettes last night. How does that happen when I haven't smoked in over seven years? My saintly wife made oatmeal and coffee for me...and then ran around with me.

I got to Jeanne's place at around 4:45, loaded up her bike, and we were off. We had to park in a different parking lot than usual, as we knew the Sports Basement would be packed. We found a cop, and asked if we could park in the lot we chose, thus avoiding a fourth ticket on this adventure.

The good folks at ALC had us arrive an hour and a half early so we could sign in, turn in pledges, attach our numbers to our bikes and stick them on our helmets. The whole process took about five minutes. Oh well... We had plenty of time to socialize with old friends. It's really funny that these folks, all of whom I've known for less than seven months, would be old friends, but that's honestly how it feels.

First we saw Shelly and Alan. It was hard to miss them. Alan was wearing a huge chicken head hat and a bright yellow feather boa. I'm beginning to suspect he may be a homosexual.

Alan always seems to be there when we need someone to cheer us on.

Shelly was wearing a huge headdress of black and white feathers, and a black and white polka dot skirt, perfect attire for that hundred plus mile ride. I always suspected she might be a lunatic, suspicions were confirmed when she started babbling about double centuries and death rides. Shelly was with me on my first training ride, and in spirit she will be with me on every ride I do.

I saw George Harrison, who was my first face to face contact with ALC. He is the nicest man, another hug, but compared to Shelly and Alan, George is so reserved. He is probably as reserved as any guy who ever posed nude for a calendar. You can find George in the "Boys of ALC" calendar. I don't own it. I'm waiting for the "Girls of ALC" calendar to come out, but I suspect it will be a very long wait. I would, however, be willing to shoot all the pictures, and of course all proceeds would go to ALC. Yes, it would be a huge sacrifice, but that's just the kind of guy I am.

We saw Stephanie the cute, young Ride Leader whom we'd all follow to the ends of the earth, unless of course, some stranger should point in another direction. We saw Ben, the crazy Brit who bets on how many miles Jeanne and I will get out before one of us has some kind of mechanical breakdown. We saw the twins, Court and Kate, with a few other younger ladies. Apparently they are multiplying. They're the nice, beautiful, young, sweet athletic, strong girls who make me feel old, and ask me for jokes every time they pass by.

We saw Julie Brown, who was my first ride leader. She really encouraged me to sign up, and guided me through my first ride, along with Shelly. She sang "High Hopes" to me the first time I did the Sausalito Hill, and no matter how many times

Shelly told her to "shut the fuck up," Julie just kept belting it out.

There were 600 riders for Day on The Ride. That's a pretty good-sized chunk of humanity. I have to say this may very well be the finest group of people I have ever been associated with, and I'm very proud to be a part of them.

Before we left everybody did their stretching and then Stephen Cadby, Associate Director of the AIDS/LifeCycle, spoke. He really touched me when he had us all hold hands, Jeanne on my left and Nicole on my right, and he spoke about getting involved.

He said some people see suffering and they just watch, and some people get involved and do something about it, and his point, and I guess mine too, is people who get involved at great personal sacrifice are heroes. Then he said the person whose hand you are holding is a hero. I don't know what Nicole and Jeanne have put aside to do this ride, but I'm willing to bet they could spend a week's vacation a lot more comfortably than they will on a little skinny bicycle seat and sleeping on the ground in a tent.

I don't know what else they do on their weekends, but week in and week out, Sunday after Sunday I've seen them sweat their asses off, up hill after hill, steeper and longer each week, in order to be ready for this ride. And so I was thinking these two women, whose hands I was holding, really were heroes, and I was really proud to be holding their hands when he said that, and then, at exactly the same moment, Nicole and Jeanne squeezed my hands. It was a really special moment in my life.

Jeanne started crying she was so moved, or maybe she was just scared of the 100 plus miles to come. I asked if she was crying, and she told me I hadn't seen anything yet, to wait for the real ride.

We all mounted up (I just love saying that) and we departed in groups of 200 or so. Jeanne and I were in the second group and before long I was passing more folks than she. I waited for her at the end of the Golden Gate at the top of the hill where I always wait for her. That was the last time I waited. The rest of the day, and every hill, was hers. She had a great ride!

We were pumped with adrenaline and I was overjoyed by the near perfect weather. The winds were light, and whereas the forecast had called for rain in the morning, it was just a gorgeous day. We climbed Camino Alto faster than ever, and it felt as though we were flying through the small towns.

Day on the Ride is set up like a regular day on the ride, hence the name "Day on the Ride." Is that ingenious or what!? So there are rest stops, complete with snacks, drinks, and port-a-potties. Rest Stop 1 was staffed by the Positive Peddlers. When I first heard about them, I thought it was like an Optimist Club on bicycles. The Positive Peddlers, in fact, are a group of people who are HIV positive, and are dedicated to raising awareness and participating in HIV and AIDS fundraising rides. They may, in fact, be optimistic, but for me "courageous" is the first word that comes to mind when describing them.

The Rest Stop had a tropical theme and many of the guys were dressed in grass skirts with coconut shell bras. Jeanne thought they looked great, but sadly, there were no women dressed in this attire.

We got some snacks, refilled water bottles, and now joined by Dellma, Jeanne's friend who was planning on driving back with us from L.A., we quickly hit the road. We were still feeling great, and seeing we left at least a hundred people behind us at Rest Stop 1, most of whom were in line for the bathrooms, we knew we weren't last yet.

The next rest stop was at Sammy Pee (Samuel P. Taylor Park). We now call it Sammy Pee because it is our restroom of choice, and while those other hundred folks were wriggling in line at Rest Stop 1, we were counting on Sammy Pee.

Taylor Park, Day on The Ride

We zoomed through Fairfax, and hit White's Hill. Jeanne passed me easily, but I'm okay with that. She's worked hard to be the stronger climber, and I'm proud of her for doing it. Besides, it's a ride, not a race.

We flew down the other side of White's Hill, and we kept a clip of near twenty mph for the next five miles or so. We made it into the bathrooms in a breeze. We saw Stephanie and a couple of others there. Then we rode through Sammy Pee on the bike trail, and quickly arrived at Rest Stop 2, which was gaily decorated in a rainbow motif.

I've mentioned before I think Sammy Pee is one of the nicest places on earth, with its majestic redwoods, and incredible canopy of green. Seeing these beautiful faces at Rest Stop 2 only enhanced it, but we had to keep going. I refilled again, with fruit punch and water. When I returned, Jeanne was conversing with Psycho Alan, and I had to pry her away to keep us moving.

There's something I have to confess, something I tend to say no matter what the task or obstacle. This may explain why my youngest daughter, Katelyn, would be laughing at her teachers every time they said "Do it," in elementary school. Whether it is getting ready to mow a lawn, or whatever the task I'll say, "Let's do it!" and then I add "Or we could just mow the lawn." Sometimes it's good for a chuckle.

Sometimes, however, I forget my audience, and as we were departing Sammy Pee with Court and Kate and all the other nice, beautiful, young, athletic, strong, sweet girls who make me feel old I said, "Let's do it!" and then added "or we could just ride our bicycles!" Wow! No chuckle here let me tell you. My comment was greeted with a loud chorus of "EWWWWW!" as if the entire group had simultaneously stepped in something nasty. I was horribly embarrassed and of course, I should have been.

We passed the twins and other youngsters on the way out of the park, and I asked Jeanne if she thought it might be good if I apologized, and she thought it was no big deal, and if it was a big deal, I might just be digging myself in deeper if I apologized. When the twins and their buddies passed us again at the first tough grade, as they always do, they asked if I had any good jokes today, so I guess they weren't that offended.

Up until this point the ride had been easy, but all of a sudden I found myself struggling, running out of gas as it were. I knew we had the Cheese Factory Hill just ahead of us, and I asked Jeanne if we might stop for a while to do a Gu shot. We invited Dellma to join us, and we knew there was a convenient place to stop up ahead as Tonto...err...Jeanne remembered last week we had seen a couple of guys pull over in a car to hit a crack pipe. We stopped, did our shots (it was Dellma's first), hydrated, and in a couple of minutes we were riding again. Sometimes a couple of minutes rest is all it takes to get you back in gear.

When we hit the Cheese Factory Hill, which is one of the toughest I've ever done, Dellma, and then Jeanne both passed me. Dellma was soon out of sight, and then Jeanne disappeared as well. I was in a good place though, kind of enjoying the rhythm, and watching the scenery pass by slowly. As I was riding I starting singing, and a beautiful young lady on a mountain bike pulled up along side and asked what I was singing, which I guess says something about my singing. Then she asked if we could sing something together, and we did. She rode with me all the way to the Cheese Factory, even after I reunited with Jeanne. What a nice kid!

She was badly in need of a saddle and if, per chance, she's reading this, I still have one for her if she gets in touch with me (MeanOldDaddy@aol.com). 585 miles is a long way to ride on a seat full of duct tape, but I have no doubt she'll make it, with or without a new saddle. When we arrived at the Cheese Factory, I noticed some folks had already opted for a turn back to Point Reyes from Sammy Pee, and others were debating whether to head back from here so as to avoid the Marshall Wall. For Jeanne and I there was no option. We were bound and determined to do the hundred plus miles. Jeanne powdered her nose with some of the other womenfolk, as womenfolk are wont to do. While I was waiting I met Dave Ellison, who I have corresponded with by e-mail many times, but have never met in person. He is such a nice man, a teacher and a columnist in our local paper.

I had a couple of snacks and again refilled my bottles. It was great finally meeting Dave, but once again, all too soon, it was time to ride out and head for the Marshall Wall.

The ride to the wall seemed quick, and was a constant game of cat and mouse, with Jeanne and Dellma putting ground between us on every uphill, and me catching up on all the downhills.

There was a water stop at the base of the Marshall Wall, and we stopped and procrastinated with other riders. The twins were there, and their friends. The atmosphere was a bit tense before the massive hill, and there was a lot of nervous joking and laughter. We psyched up like everybody else, and hit it.

My strategy on this hill, as with every other, is to ride slowly and steadily, but never stop or walk. With my heart troubles, I really feel like I have nothing to prove to anyone on the hills, and my dear friend Jeanne will wait for me somewhere ahead, as I would for her.

So Dellma was off like a flash, and soon Jeanne was out far enough ahead that I was able to take a very distant photo of a side view of her on a turn. She looks like an ant in the photo. I just kept plugging along, never stopping, enjoying the wildflowers, and even taking a few pictures of them along the way. It was some of the most enjoyable suffering I have ever done. Certainly the view was awe-inspiring.

Jeanne waited for me at the peak, and then we zipped down the hill until we saw the little red church which signifies you need to hit your brakes hard, or you might end up as road kill on the intersecting Highway 1 at the bottom of the hill.

We turned onto the highway and passed the scenic little town of Marshall. Lunch was scheduled in Point Reyes, and we *were ready for a break, and starving. I believe somebody added several hills since the ride the week before, or maybe we were just that hungry. Anyway, it sure seemed as though they added some and we really struggled. We looked for the dead deer from the week before, but we didn't see it. I'm pretty sure we smelled it though.*

I figured as inhospitable as the town of Point Reyes had been to me as a cyclist, there was no way they were going to be hosting any lunch for ALC's Day on The Ride. All along when folks had been discussing lunch at Point Reyes, I had presumed they were talking about the Park beyond the town.

Jeanne, however, didn't figure it that way, and she started looking for the big lunch festivities in town. She really let her imagination run wild as she got just a little anxious, okay, panicky, that we had missed the noon meal.

Jeanne is the dot in the center of the photo on a small portion of the Marshall Wall

She started babbling that even if we hadn't missed lunch, we would probably be stuck with the last three meals (we passed one guy who had blinded himself by accidentally getting sunscreen in his eyes), which indubitably would be red pepper sandwiches, and after all this time and all these miles, and all these hills, how could we possibly survive on RED PEPPER SANWICHES!?!?!? Where was lunch? How could we not see it?

For the first time in the hundreds of miles we have ridden together, I was sure Jeanne was wrong, and lunch was actually at the Pt. Reyes National Seashore Park, a few more miles away. I almost had to smack her to calm her down, as they do in bad movies.

Thank God we had a map or Jeanne might have had us cruising every street in that cold little town, until somebody gave us some freaking lunch, and that would have been until we dropped dead, because they don't GIVE anything to cyclists in Point Reyes. Remember, this is the town where even if you buy food in their stores or restaurants, the only way to get water is to buy it bottled and pour it into your water bottle, and after all this you have to pay to use the bathroom.

So after Jeanne pulled over and checked the map, we struggled through the three miles between the town of Point Reyes, and Point Reyes National Seashore Park, which would normally be a sprint. We finally made it to lunch. Of course there were plenty of lunches left. I knew we had passed four other riders earlier on, but I guess Jeanne had forgotten them. We caught up with Dellma there, but she was done eating. She kept us company while Jeanne and I pulled up some cardboard to keep from sitting in burrs or thorns, and we wolfed down everything in our lunches. You can't imagine how comfy cardboard can be, until you've done seventy hard, hilly, hungry miles on a skinny bike seat.

About the time we finished eating, someone came by to tell us the lunch stop was closing. We had to get moving, or get sagged (sagged...as in being picked up by a vehicle and transported either to the next rest stop or if you wish, the end of the ride). Hearing that panicked us, and we moved at an almost urgent pace.

We stopped on the way back again at Sammy P, but only for water and bathrooms. I think we were somewhat disoriented by this time. Our quick in and out turned out to be a little longer than planned as Jeanne waited for me at the restrooms, and I waited for her at the water. Yup, our team was running like a well-oiled machine!

We hit the road once more. Dellma rode on ahead, saying she wanted to get back at a decent hour so she could go to church. Somewhere between Sammy P and Lagunitas, on that horrible stretch of road where the cars tail you and the crevices want to devour you, my zipper broke on my bike pack and my camera bounced out and onto the road. I pulled over as quickly as I could, put my bike down on the side of the road, and ran back to get my new camera. I could see the wheels of the cars and trucks missing it by inches as I ran to retrieve it. Dodging traffic, I was able to snag it up, and returned to my bike.

When I got back to my bike I realized I had placed it in a lovely patch of poison oak. Worse yet, both of my water bottles had fallen from their cages and had rolled through the poison oak. I carefully picked out my bottles, returned them to their cages and we were on the road again. For the rest of the ride, I was afraid to drink from my bottles. I felt like a guy stranded on the ocean in a raft, completely surrounded by water, but unable to drink. Except of course I was on a bicycle on a road and I could pull over at one of the many restaurants along the way and order a diet coke. Eventually I succumbed and drank, but I could just feel that poison oak oil doing its thing. It's interesting how your mind will play games, especially when you're exhausted.

We had a good tailwind from Lagunitas up the backside of White's Hill, and considering we were pretty much spent, we were keeping a decent clip. Our conversations usually go something like this. The front one of us will say "How's my speed? Want me to pick it up a bit?" And the other will reply "No. No I'm good..." Sometimes we play the same kind of "counting the ceiling tiles when you're bored" games one plays when one is alone, and tired, and bored. Interestingly enough, I don't think the games are any better with two of us playing, but sometimes we get punchy, and we find ourselves very entertaining, like two teens getting high for the first time.

Earlier, at the top of the Marshall Wall, I was looking down the hill, beyond a cow pasture with a bunch of cows. From that height, sometimes the foggy sky and the ocean blend together, and you can't distinguish where one starts and the other stops. So from that vantage point it looked like there was a gargantuan domino floating in the sky. I pointed and asked Jeanne what it was, and she replied "a cow." I thought this was hysterical, and the only one in the whole world who could ever, and in fact did think it was funnier than I did, was Jeanne.

We decided we would ride through the last rest stop in Fairfax, and then stop at our regular Gu shot stop just before Camino Alto. There were lots of folks at the rest stop who waved as we rode by. If they all didn't pass us on the final two hills, we wouldn't be last. We made it over Camino Alto, and it gets to be less strain, even with more miles behind us, every week. Jeanne once again left me in the dust, but I caught her on the downhill. Several more riders passed us both.

We stopped momentarily at Mike's Bikes to refill water containers. I knew one of my containers had gone drinking spout first in the poison oak, and the other had just touched it at the bottom of the bottle. Now I couldn't remember which was which, and I was sure my tongue, lips and face would be a massive, swollen, oozing rash in a few days.

Finally we came to the Sausalito Hill, TLFH. At the end of every ride, once we get up that hill, I'm rejuvenated and it's a sprint to the finish at the Sports Basement. Of course, it doesn't hurt that it's all downhill from there.

The Sports Basement looked exceptionally wonderful today, and as Jeanne said "rounding that corner into the Sports Basement parking lot has never been sweeter!" Alan and Edna cheered us in with pom-poms and everyone else stood and cheered for us. Many of my friends and mentors were there to greet me. Alan and Edna both gave me a big hug and a smooch, and then Shelly came and gave me a big hug and a smooch on the cheek as well. I know she had a lot of visits to do (she's a pet sitter) but she waited to leave so she could cheer me in. That meant a lot to me.

Julie Brown gave me a big hug too. She has such a huge heart in that tiny little body. It was so great that all of the folks who guided me along, step by step, could be here to share the completion of my first century. Jeanne and I signed in, parked our bikes in the bike valet parking (how cool is that?!) and then grabbed a plate full of incredibly good food. We sat on the curb and ate our celebratory meal and cheered the other riders in. WE WEREN'T EVEN CLOSE to last. The first rider who came in after us was greeted with huge cheers just like ours, plus two additional voices. Jeanne and I exchanged a secret glance which whispered "we're not last" and continued our meal. The next couple of riders came in and the glance we exchanged maybe said, "hmmm that's a pleasant surprise." By the time many more riders came rolling in, Jeanne and I were absolutely high-fiving with our eyes! Well not literally, cause that would really hurt, but we were definitely proud to be sitting on that curb with our plates of spaghetti cheering other riders in, and every time our eyes met, we were almost giddy. I kept thinking "oh my God oh my God oh my God WE DID IT!"

So in one week short of a year, 358 days, I went from riding four blocks and hurting, to riding 104 miles... and hurting. It took eight hours and 30 minutes, and we averaged 12.2 mph. Lydia says "we rock!" Jeanne says "we're ready!" I say a big thank you to all of you who helped me get to this point...You know who you are...You know what we should do? We should all ride our bikes to L.A...Nah! That would be crazy!

3,400 miles thus far in my training

Shiv's Story

A few weeks ago, I met a woman named Shiv on the Cat II ride, but I know I'd seen her around. Shiv is a pretty memorable character, starting with her hot pink dreadlocks. If the dreads aren't enough to make you remember her, she also has the most beautiful English accent. We were riding along, some conversation occurred and she, and her road partner Kate, introduced themselves.

As I often do whenever I meet someone new on a training ride, I went home and looked up Kate's and Shiv's homepages. Kate's wasn't too wordy, but Shiv (like me) has written a novel on her homepage. It was interesting reading.

I gathered from her page that Shiv had walked out on a $165,000 annual salary as a lawyer, to start a new life wherein she struggles along financially, but is much more fulfilled spiritually.

Later, I learned Shiv's decision to leave the legal profession came one night when a friend called her at her law office after he learned he was HIV positive. She wanted to be there for him, but was committed to reviewing a stack of legal documents. She made a conscious decision a job would never again keep her from a friend who was in that much pain.

I also gather from reading Shiv's page she is very serious about yoga, and (at least) seriously influenced by Hinduism. At one point on her homepage she says:

> *"Yoji Bhajan always reminded us that: We are Spiritual Beings here for a human experience... not human beings here for a Spiritual experience."*

I had a similar experience to Shiv's, though much less dramatic. Some refer to it as "cashing out." I left a position as a program director for a non-profit organization, to be a gardener. My dad was thrilled, and told me I was going backwards three generations.

At the time of the knife "incident" where I cut the straps for a fellow outside of the Sausalito Soccer field bathroom, I asked Shiv about her decision to leave the legal profession. I asked if she was happy.

After reading her homepage, I guess I was expecting some wise mystical answer from Shiv. Maybe she would tell me something about the riches her spiritual being was enjoying, or maybe something about the importance of feeding the soul. Whatever I was expecting, Shiv simply replied, "Fuck yeah!"

May 22, 2005 Petaluma (and beyond)

Today's ride was scheduled for 90 miles, it was the thirteenth, and the last ride in the Cat II series set up by our ride leader, Ben Armstrong (whom Jeanne now calls the New Marquis de Sade). Others have been calling this ride the "Ben Armstrong Every Fucking Hill In Marin Ride," but I thought we should just call it the "Ben Armstrong EFHIM" ride for short.

Jeanne and I had ridden about 42 miles the day before in an invigorating ride through Fremont and Milpitas. We did some climbing, going a ways up Calaveras Road to Ed Levin Park. It was a smooth ride. I flatted once, but (shock) Jeanne never did.

I have really grown to love my friend and riding partner, Jeanne. I feel so fortunate to have found her, and I believe that, as so many others who have helped me along in this endeavor, she was sent to me by God to help guide me along this sojourn. Having said that, sometimes I wonder WHY I feel that way...

Everything went really smoothly...until we started riding. It looked like we were going to get a good jump on the pack, as Jeanne and I were riding and others were still walking to their bikes, but within a block Jeanne called out "Stopping!" and she pulled over. Her cycle computer wasn't registering, and she made adjustments. The computer really isn't necessary. It's not like the computer in a car. It has nothing whatsoever to do with the functionality of the bike. It has an odometer, a tripometer, a speedometer, and it keeps track of your maximum speed, average speed, and riding time. Mine has a cadence counter which keeps track of my pedaling rpm's, and then it has an arrow indicator which tells whether you are riding over or under your average speed. Jeanne's is the only cycle computer in the world which has a wind meter. Mostly though, the function of the cycle computer is that it gives you something to play with when you're on a really long ride and you're bored.

So in a very short time, just about the time it took for nearly the entire group to mount up and pass us, Jeanne had her computer functioning again and we were off like a shot, albeit a very slow shot. But it's okay that we lost so much time, because Jeanne's my friend, and friends stop and wait for each other. God knows she's waited for me often enough without complaint.

Although the Sports Basement opens early so we can use their restrooms, we left before they arrived, just before 7:00 AM, so we weren't able to use the facilities. Jeanne and I, and many others, were in desperate need, and we remembered a restroom on the near side of Sausalito about five miles away. We were pretty motivated to get there quickly, and once we arrived, we were horribly disappointed to find the bathrooms closed for cleaning.

We knew there was another public restroom on the far side of Sausalito at the soccer fields, and so now we were off like a (faster now) shot again. We made the bathrooms without any accidents, and that was pretty much the best thing that happened all day. When we got back to our bikes, Jeanne debated whether she (read "I") should adjust her cleats now, or wait until we rolled into Fairfax. I could go either way, but I didn't want to take the time to debate it.

So we moved on. Camino Alto truly gets easier every week and we got to the top together in no time. When we got to Fairfax, we had a couple of Clif bars, and I adjusted Jeanne's cleats. Of course I was happy to do it, because Jeanne's my friend, and friends do that kind of thing for each other. When Ben arrived we knew we were behind because Ben was sweeping. We left right away.

Jeanne beat me up White's Hill by a small piece, but the downhill and flat after are the best anywhere, so I knew I'd pass her and gain some ground for the next hill and I wouldn't get so far behind. But Jeanne had other plans. Her calf was hurting. We had to pull over and readjust her cleat again. Of course I didn't mind at all. That's what friends are for. We then continued on over the dreaded Nicasio Hill (with Jeanne leaving me in the dust) to Nicasio, where we stopped briefly.

While we were there at the little store in town, a small stake bed truck pulled into the lot, and in the back was a young fawn. It had been badly injured, and I was really heartbroken to see it in such agony. I was really in a hurry to move on, as to me there's nothing worse than watching something or someone suffer, and being helpless to do anything about it. But we needed to re- readjust Jeanne's cleat.

We did the five or so mile stretch to the Cheese Factory Hill at a good clip. It was pretty windy, and Jeanne commented that if we had this kind of wind in the morning, the afternoon would be a mess. The ever optimistic Ms. McArthur then headed up the hill, and she quickly passed me. Before long I looked up to see her walking along carrying her front wheel off the ground. The road is very narrow, and there is no shoulder. It's a road which is frequented by RVs and SUVs pulling huge trailers. Sometimes I swear I can feel them brushing the hair on my arms, but I think it's just the wind they create coming so close at such high speeds. So Jeanne had to carry her bike up to the next turnout. I arrived just about the same time, pulled over, and we changed the tire. I was happy to help her…after all, what kind of a friend would I be if I just left her behind?

We have a disagreement every time we fix a flat. I always think we should inflate the tire more, risking breaking the valve stem in the pumping process, but having a firm tire when I get done. Jeanne always thinks an under-inflated tire is better than a broken stem, but an under-inflated tire is also more prone to getting a flat. I guess we were both proven right eventually, and so the debate will rage on.

About one pump after Jeanne told me it was good enough, and the tire felt fine, I broke the valve stem, and we started the process all over again. About this time Ben and Joseph pulled up, and there we were, dead last. Once we got back on the road, Jeanne, with her now under-inflated tire, was off like a bat out of hell, leaving me in sole possession of the not so coveted, last place. I hate being last, but I know Jeanne would pretty much do anything that wasn't immoral or illegal for me, so I sucked it up.

About ten minutes later, Joseph pulled over with a woman taking Claritin, and Ben rode down the hill, I think just because he wanted to ride back up. I was no longer last...by one. Good enough for me!

We stayed at the Cheese Factory long enough to refill bottles and powder noses. There were about 20 riders here still, and Jeanne and I took off while they were still resting. We were soon riding in uncharted territory for us. The road was called "Wilson Hill Road." We took it as a bad sign that they would put the word "hill" in the road name, and our prediction proved true. While the hill was not as long as the Marshall Wall, it was steeper in places. It's been a while since I was riding 2.9 mph up a hill, the minimum speed I can ride uphill without falling over, but here I was just barely making that pace.

The scenery on Wilson Hill was as beautiful as the ride was difficult. I would have enjoyed it even more had there not been hundreds of caterpillars crawling across the road, as I was keeping an eye out for them trying not to squish anyone. When we finally hit the summit the view was spectacular! Kurt was there taking it all in, so Jeanne and I pulled over with him. We were soon joined by three more riders and then, to my horror, Ben pulled up to tell us we were being "swept." But there were so many riders back at the Cheese Factory, how could we be last? Ben explained the others had all made the decision to turn back to San Francisco.

I looked at the other riders around me. Jeanne has been consistently taking me on every hill. She used to be hesitant on the downhills and I could always catch and pass her there, but lately, she's been throwing caution to the wind and staying right with me, even as I'm riding around 35 mph. The rest of the riders are younger, stronger, and thinner. I resigned myself to the idea that when we reached Petaluma for lunch, I'd be receiving the Special Olympic cheers.

So we were off again, me, and then Ben sweeping at the rear of the pack. Ben talked about the countryside in the U.K., and how it was always green. I asked him about the rest of the ride to Petaluma, or "Petalumer," as he says with his British accent. He said it was just a few more miles, and assured me we had ridden the last hill in. Then, about two miles before "Petalumer," we came to another good-sized hill. I told him that I thought he had told me the previous hill was the last one before lunch, to which he replied simply, "I lied."

We arrived at lunch in a very nice little café in Petaluma. I took my bows upon receiving the thunderous ovation I so richly deserved for being last, and then we ordered lunch. There was a lovely piece of hot Lasagna with my name on it. Jeanne asked if I knew what I was having and I pointed out the lasagna. Jeanne looked at everything but the lasagna saying "that looks good" and "Oh! That looks great!" My mom raised me as a gentleman, and as such I allowed Jeanne to go ahead and order first, and when she did, she asked for the last piece of Lasagna. So a cold turkey sandwich looked okay too. I was happy my friend could enjoy the lasagna...ahem.

We ate quickly, hoping we could get out in time to keep from being last. The twins, along with another friend, were getting ready to leave, and I thought if we hurried we could follow them. Tonto McArthur wanted to take a quick look at her map, and so the triplets were soon out of sight. There was a fellow ALCer waiting at a light, and he pointed us in a direction, we rode a little piece and then Tonto whipped out the map one more time, just to make sure. She picked a course and we were on the road again.

There was nothing to indicate it on the map, but Ben had mentioned a hill coming out of Petaluma, almost in passing, after the safety speech. Jeanne and I were riding up a hill, but when we crossed over the summit, I knew there was no way this was any hill worth Ben's mentioning, and I told Jeanne as much. I asked her how confident she was in her orienteering, and she was "very confident." After about three miles, we came to a point in the rode where we had two choices. Either we could take the on ramp to Highway 101 toward San Francisco, or we could go the wrong way on the off ramp from highway 101, against traffic, toward San Francisco. Neither seemed like a very good choice, and certainly neither was the correct route. Jeanne apologized, but what the heck, friends sometimes get friends lost, after they eat the last piece of lasagna...it happens, sometimes (grrrrrr!)

In all honesty, were the orienteering left to me, we might be in another state by now. I really have no room to complain here. It was just the combination of unfortunate events which had me frustrated...and exhausted!

So we turned around into a hellacious headwind and rode back the three miles to wherever the hell it was, and got back on the right road...maybe. Well probably, because Jeanne was...err...sort of confident...sort of.

The next eight and one half miles were the worst I ever spent on a bicycle, and that's saying something, because now I've ridden well over 3,500 miles getting prepared for ALC 4. We had headwinds, and crosswinds and every kind of wind but a tailwind. I'm not exaggerating when I say it was over six miles uphill. Every time we thought it had to end, it just kept going, and the higher we went, the steeper it got. It was the most seriously I ever considered walking, and what made it even worse was that we weren't sure we were even on the right road.

We had not seen any other riders since Petaluma, and darn few cars for that matter. The half hour we spent on our little detour to highway 101 had us not only in last place, but likely put us behind the sweeps. We decided if, and when we hit the summit of this hill, we'd scout around, and if nothing looked familiar, we'd coast back down the hill into Petaluma, and call Jerie, Jeanne's sister, to come and pick us up. It sounded like a good plan, but when we got to the peak, and there wasn't anything familiar, Jeanne just coasted down the hill away from Petaluma. I followed her, knowing if we found nothing, we would have to ride back up and over. This was NOT our agreed upon plan!

Somewhere on the way down though, I noticed familiar looking caterpillars and I figured we had to be in the same neighborhood as Wilson Hill, somewhere near the Cheese Factory. Shortly thereafter, Jeanne said she felt like the "T" (well actually she called it a "Y" but it's a "T") to Marshall should be coming along anytime, and this time, she was right.

We saw the flag at the fire station next to the Cheese Factory, and we knew we were almost there... to the Cheese Factory that is, leaving us with a mere forty or so miles to go.

When we arrived at the Cheese Factory, the only people remaining were the triplets (the twins plus one now), Ben, and Joseph. They all wanted to know how we got behind the sweeps, and how we got lost, and how many extra miles we traveled.

Joseph kindly said he had wanted to get a soda, and so we had plenty of time to rest. He was really on his way out, but he didn't want us to feel badly for making him wait with us. I had to refill my bottles, as I had sucked out every last drop going up that horrible hill. I was also feeling pretty sore, and so I asked Jeanne for my butt butter, which she had been carrying in her backpack.

Jeanne offered to fill my bottles while I used the facilities, and said she would need the butt butter after me, "Is that okay?"

Maybe it should have struck me funny that Jeanne would ask to use my butt butter. It's not something you would ever think anyone would ask. What struck me as funny, though, was that she'd even ask at all, after all we'd been through together, and the many miles, sharing butt butter should be a given.

Soon we were off. The triplets were out with at least a ten minute head start. I felt a bit better after the break, and I knew once we hit the summit of the Cheese Factory Hill, I'd at least have another break on the downhill. Jeanne, as usual, was ahead of me on the hill, but I nearly caught her on the downhill. By the time we made the left turn on Nicasio Valley Road, I was with her again.

We had a great tailwind, and made quick time running between twenty and twenty-five mph for almost five miles. Jeanne made the left into Nicasio, and I passed by the town, so I was actually ahead of her going toward the Nicasio Hill. Jeanne told me there were three riders in Nicasio, which meant if we could keep ahead of them we wouldn't be last.

I forgot this hill could be a struggle. The fact that I set my all-time speed record going in the reverse direction a few weeks ago (42 mph) should have been a clue. There are two summits to this road. I could see the three riders from Nicasio approaching from the rear. They couldn't have been three feet behind me when I hit the first peak, and I put enough distance between them and myself that I was barely able to hold them off until the second peak, and I gained more ground on them. Did I mention I hate being last?

So we rolled onto Sir Francis Drake Blvd., going up the reverse of White's Hill, and the three riders from Nicasio passed me. Jeanne put serious distance between us too, and after the summit she was completely out of sight. I caught her as we were making good time through the back streets of Fairfax. By the time we came to Broadway in Fairfax, we had caught the three riders from Nicasio, and we even passed the triplets! Hills are a weakness for Jeanne, and even more so for me, but we can ride with almost anyone on the flats, and there was a lot of flat ground between Broadway and Camino Alto. Not only that, but I'm not that much slower than anybody else on Camino Alto, so maybe I could hold them all off until Sausalito!

We had passed two more riders in Fairfax, the three riders from Nicasio, and now I was passing the triplets like they were standing still. They even asked how I could possibly ride so fast after so many miles. I was feeling really good, and nothing could stop me now. And then I thought I heard someone calling...no...no...I don't think I did. I must be imagining...and then one of the triplets picked up her pace and nearly caught me and yelled "Hey! Slow down! This is a residential neighborhood!" and then she said "Your wife needs you!" I was wondering how she could possibly have been in contact with my wife, and then I realized she was talking about Jeanne.

I was explaining that Jeanne and I weren't married and that my wife was at home...but she interrupted and said "I don't know about that, Jeanne just said 'Oh! Shit! Go get Russ!'" I expected Jeanne would be right behind me, so I was surprised I had to ride back nearly a mile to reach her. She had already removed her tire and the old tube. I took over, and Jeanne explained she had hit a pot hole really hard and the tube popped. I was thinking if the tube had been properly inflated, we would be riding over Camino Alto. While I was thinking this and finishing up with the tire, the riders from Nicasio, and then the riders from Fairfax passed by, and soon, Ben and Joseph were there.

We were last, again. I was heartbroken. There was no way I'd catch anyone now, with Camino Alto looming. Still, Jeanne and I discussed it, and I knew after I rode back all that way, and helped with her tire, Jeanne wouldn't make me suffer the indignity of riding last alone and I was comforted by that.

We rode all the way to Camino Alto together, and headed up the hill. Yup, even though she's stronger on the hills, there's no way my pal Jeanne would ride off and leave me alone riding last. That's exactly what I was thinking as she rode out of sight over Camino Alto...

I caught Jeanne at the traffic light at the base of the hill. She was talking with another ALC rider, and we passed him before we came to the soccer fields. We really poured it on all the way through Sausalito. We stopped at Mike's Bike just long enough to get a half a bottle of water, and that's all the water I would need to get up TLFH. I told Jeanne I really didn't want to do this hill, and she reminded me this would be the last time this season that I would have to ride it. It made it much easier, and I really tried to take it all in and enjoy it.

As I was riding, I realized how fortunate I was to have the opportunity to ride this hill, and enjoy the wild flowers, and the beauty of the structure of the bridge as it came into view. In fact, every hill I've ridden has a beauty all its own, and even though they're a pain in the ass, I guess they're worth it...kind of like Jeanne.

We flew across the Golden Gate, down the hill, and into the lot of the Sports Basement. We were so late, there was hardly anyone around to welcome us.

We signed out, and as I was signing I decided I would wait and cheer for the last rider, but as I was writing the last seven on my rider number I heard Jeanne clap and say "YAY!"

We rode ninety-six miles on our ninety mile ride.

3,537 miles thus far in my training

Jeanne's Wind Indicator

Early on in our riding together, I installed a cycle computer on Jeanne's bike. One day when we were riding back into Mill Valley and Sausalito against a hellacious headwind, Jeanne commented that the winds were going crazy, first going one direction, and then the complete opposite.

I was kind of shocked by this, as from where I was sitting, the wind was only blowing one direction, and that was straight into our faces. But Jeanne was very sure it was changing, first being a tailwind and then a head wind, because it said so on her "wind indicator." I thought it was strange that she would carry a wind indicator while riding, until she told me it was built into her cycle computer.

The cycle computer keeps track of your average speed, and has a little arrow indicator which lets you know whether you're riding over, or under your average mph, or, if you're Jeanne, it's a wind indicator.

There have been many times when I have turned to Jeanne for help to keep me from looking foolish or ignorant when I'm lost in situations unfamiliar to me. It seems unfair that I should exploit the one area in which she is unfamiliar, to have a laugh at her expense. But what the hell...she ate the last piece of lasagna!

May 29, 2005 Training Journal Entry

This was the last training ride...the Margarita ride. Today was more of a celebration than a ride. Jeanne and I parked on Bay Street and rode to the Sports Basement. We then departed for a quick sprint to Guaymas in Tiburon for breakfast and margaritas.

Everything about this ride was perfect. The weather was perfect, there were lots of "old" friends to socialize with, and I felt great!

I don't know if it was intentional, but this ride was a great psychological boost. You see, it was only a few months ago this little sprint, and it literally was a sprint, was a half of a ride. It wasn't that long ago that I struggled with this ride, and the small "hills" along the way. Today, I felt like I was flying and they weren't really hills at all. It's funny how your definitions change and everything is relative.

Jeanne and I were riding very near the front of the pack at the halfway point, but when we hit the stoplight beyond the soccer fields in Sausalito, Jeanne told me she promised to wait here for Jane, so I waited with her.

Breakfast was great. We honored Ben Armstrong, our Training Ride Leader who set up the CAT II series, to include what the riders affectionately term "Every Fucking Hill in Marin", or EFHIM. We gave him an old cut-off Tiki torch. Ben is British, and he sent us all a list of items which we would need for camp. Among those items, Ben listed a "torch," which we discerned is British for "flashlight." As we are forever harassing him for his use of British terms like "refuse bin" and "rubbish" and such, the award seemed appropriate.

After breakfast, we all hopped on a ferry, another first for me, and headed back to the city by way of Angel Island and Alcatraz. On the ferry ride over, we all reminisced about past rides, and in so doing, we talked about the time Jeanne flatted on White's Hill, and, because of her flat I was able to take the pictures of the turkeys. Jeanne, perhaps in retaliation for all of the teasing in my ride journal, casually asked, "You mean the time you got the turkey porn?"

I made a feeble attempt to stop the conversation right there by telling her it was merely pictures of turkeys, and at the time we saw the turkeys having sexual relations, I was unable to take a picture. This is not a group to let comments like this slide by unnoticed.

George Harrison, who is a psychiatrist, asked in his best shrink tone, "But you did want to take pictures?"

Before I could answer, George asked, "How long have you had this desire for turkey pornography?" The crowd was howling now.

Sue Lackey piped in, "When you're talking about turkey porn, I don't think it's called 'a desire.' I believe it would be called 'a hankering."

I tried once more to change the conversation. We talked about the ride to Petaluma and beyond, and how Jeanne got us lost. I told the story of Jeanne getting the last piece of lasagna and how I got stuck with a cold turkey sandwich...

George interrupted me, and assuming his psychiatrist role he said "Ah! It all comes back to the turkey once again..."

We were all nearly doubled up with laughter. It was a great trip, and a wonderful ending to our training season.

I hope I'm ready for the ride. Of course I have serious doubts and worries. But then, even veteran riders who've done the ride many times have their worries. It's no small undertaking.

Without even having pushed a pedal toward the ride, this has already been the adventure of a lifetime for me. When I think of all of the things I have seen, from the incredible views of the Golden Gate Bridge and the City skyline, to the majestic hills along the Marshall Wall, I'm pretty overwhelmed by it all. I've enjoyed a million wild flowers, and Lord knows I had plenty of time to do so as I rode 2.9 mph up so many hills. I've ridden among the sheep at Los Vaqueros Dam, and alongside foxes at the Don Edwards Wildlife Refuge. I've seen deer and quail, pheasants, ducks and geese, pelicans and sea lions, and let's not forget the turkeys.

I've ridden to cities I've never visited before, like Sausalito, Tiburon, and Fairfax, and tiny towns I've never even heard of, like Lagunitas, Nicasio, and Marshall. I've pushed myself up hills I never dreamed I would, or even could. If I'm not ready now, I never will be.

3,582 miles thus far in my training

For some folks, fundraising is the easiest part of the ALC challenge. All riders are required to raise a minimum of $2,500. I've heard one gentleman has a group of golf buddies who all agree to be part of a lottery. He puts all their names in a hat, and the first five names he pulls pledge $500. That sounds like a great plan to me!

It's a great plan unless you don't have that many friends who are able to commit to a $500 donation. I don't have one friend who can commit to $500, and that's probably true for most of the participants in ALC. I was dreading fundraising, but as it turned out, every donation renewed and reinforced my faith in humanity and so, fundraising was really an uplifting experience for me. I was stunned at the generosity of my acquaintances, friends, family, business associates, and total strangers.

It was very difficult for me to ask people for money. I had to keep reminding myself it wasn't as if I was asking for help with my house payment or to buy a new car. I truly believe in what ALC and their beneficiaries are doing.

I started my fundraising by sending an e-mail to everyone on my e-mail list...and I do mean *everyone*. I sent e-mails to people I'd never met, but with whom I'd had contact in an online health and fitness bulletin board. Many from this board gave so generously, I just couldn't believe it! One young lady, Elizabeth Ann, made a small donation of $5.00 which was kind enough, but then she made a point of reminding the other folks of my endeavor. I'm sure her prodding helped me immensely.

Another young friend of mine donated, and sent an e-mail to everyone in her address book. Her aunt, whom I had never met, also made a donation.

I sent e-mails to an online group which shares an interest in a car that I drive. I was shocked to receive a donation from this group, but very grateful.

I sent e-mails to customers, former customers, and even customers whom I left with a not-so-friendly departure. One of these former customers contributed $50 to the cause, so I guess the long shot was worth taking. Many of my gardening customers were very generous, giving $25, $50, and even $100 donations. One family said they had recently lost a dear friend to AIDS and contributed $200. I was pretty overwhelmed.

Additionally, with every e-mail communication I made, I would add a signature which said "On June 5, 2005, I will be riding my bicycle 585 miles, from San Francisco to Los Angeles, to help fight AIDS." Then I would add a tag which would direct the reader to my AIDS/LifeCycle homepage. I added this signature in my business and personal e-mails.

One time I was corresponding with a guy about purchasing a car from him. I didn't buy the car, but he saw my little plea and sent $20.

I also contacted every business which I patronize on a consistent basis. I wrote to my insurance lady, the company where I buy my gardening equipment, the lady who cuts my hair, and my auto parts guy. I even contacted my jeweler because over the years I've spent tens of dollars there, and I knew they would desperately want to keep my business.

In all seriousness, Milpitas Mowers in Milpitas, and Hair Care and Kasaria Jewelers in Newark, CA were all very generous, and they are all very good at what they do.

Instead of Christmas cards, I sent "begging letters" explaining that I only had money for postage for one or the other. Nobody complained, and some friends wrote back thanking me for helping with this very important cause, sending along a nice donation.

I talked about the ride at every opportunity, with anyone who would listen. Once, while Jeanne and I were riding, we stopped at a Subway for lunch. The lady ahead of me in line commented on our riding attire, and we explained that we were training for ALC. She wrote out a $20 check right there.

Of course I sent e-mails to all my friends. I have some really great friends, and they all came through for me. I guess I expected they might donate something, but I had no idea how generous they would all be, without exception! This was quite literally shocking to me and I will never forget how they rallied around me, offering not only financial support, but also showing a genuine interest in my training, the cause, and the event itself.

I knew my family would be there for me, as they always have been, and always will be. When I had a heart attack, my brother the counter guy, my sister the nurse, my retired Dad, my wife and my kids all mowed lawns to keep my business alive while I recovered. My Mom cooked for everybody. I knew they would support me if I was riding for the Chili Finger Defense Fund, though I suspect they might have been less generous. They all came through in a major way for the AIDS/LifeCycle.

My parents have always been generous in everything they do. When it comes to helping others, their giving spirit knows no limits. Still, I was rather surprised by the size of their contribution... and even felt a bit guilty. My Dad has never been great with names. With no malicious intent, he alternately referred to the ride as "The Gay Ride" or "The AIDS Lifestyle." But when it counted, when he handed me his donation, he got it right!

My sister Demi and her husband David are often involved in charity rides of another kind. Their motorcycle club supports various causes, but they too made a major donation. Not only that, but Demi talked me up with her friends and they were giving as well.

My daughters did their part too. They donated, their boyfriends donated, and then they helped with fundraising on their own. Erin contacted online acquaintances and business associates. Katelyn sold ALC wristbands throughout the UC Santa Cruz Campus. Megan rallied her teammates on the UC Davis Women's Rugby Team, who in some instances contacted their families to support me.

One of the sweetest donations came from a teammate of Megan's. I received a donation for a rather odd amount. Megan later told me her friend was going to make a $5.00 donation, but at the last minute decided "What the heck! It's a good cause!" and so she contributed the entire contents of her checking account, $6.50.

My brother Rick works in a rather conservative environment, to put it mildly. I wouldn't say the guys he works with are homophobic, it's just that gay people scare them. His co-workers were less than thrilled at my participation in ALC, and gave him some grief about it. I felt pretty good about his response. He told them that the AIDS/LifeCycle might not be his first choice of causes to support, but if his little brother cared about it enough to give up one of his two crappy weeks of vacation for it, then he was damn well going to contribute. Rick, and his wonderful wife Vickie, were my biggest sponsors.

I want to take this opportunity to thank all of my AIDS/LifeCycle sponsors for their help in this incredible journey. With their generosity and kindness, we surpassed the fundraising goal I had set back in October 2004. As of 7-10-2005 we raised $5,170.50. I cannot thank them enough for being a part of this! I can't thank them enough for making it possible for me to participate in this life changing experience! I can't thank them enough for caring so much!

Bike staging at the Cow Palace

The day before the ride begins, ALC sets up what they call "Day Zero." This is the day you turn in your bike, get your bike and helmet number, get your tent assignment, and in general get all your last minute ride business handled.

Shelly informed me that if you line up for your tent assignments in order, you'd end up being next-door neighbors with the person next to you in the line. I was hoping Jeanne and I could be neighbors with Shelly, who in turn was hoping to be next to Alan and Stephanie, who were also tentmates. So I arranged to meet Shelly early. Jeanne had a previous commitment first thing in the morning, so I figured I'd meet her there later and take care of all the other concerns at that time.

Shiv says it's an old Mexican proverb, "If you want to make God laugh, tell him your plans." However, many of my family members are, in fact, old Mexicans, and I've never heard any of them say this, so Shiv might be incorrect. Whoever came up with the proverb, it certainly held true for Day Zero.

I ended up working for a while in the morning, so Shelly had about given up on me and was leaving by the time I arrived. Meanwhile, Jeanne had taken care of her stuff earlier than planned, and arrived about five minutes after me. I had passed within a mile of her house on my way, and had I known she was ready to go, we could have driven in together.

ALC had everything incredibly organized. First we turned in our bikes. Volunteers put a sticker on our bikes, and on us, so we could return and attach our bike numbers once we received them.

In order to receive your bike and helmet number, you must meet your fundraising obligations, and view the safety video. We went for the safety video next.

A large group of us, maybe 300 or so, were taken into a huge viewing room where the safety video was set up and ready to roll. While we knew all of the material covered, it was still pretty entertaining and starred none other than my buddy Jeanne McArthur! Actually they filmed Jeanne riding by in one scene, but it was fun seeing her. After you've watched the entire video, you exit the room, and on your way out, you're banded. I much prefer wrist banding to the ear tagging method I've seen used on Mutual of Omaha's "Wild Kingdom."

Once you're banded you can move on to another step. We visited the financial folks next. As previously mentioned, each rider makes a commitment to raise a minimum of $2,500. Some riders simply "self pledge" the entire amount, and whip out a check or credit card on Day Zero. Other riders try to make their minimum by fundraising, but fall short. They can either choose to forget the whole thing, participate as a Roadie, or make a commitment to raise the remaining funds in 30 days. If they fail to raise the remaining funds in those 30 days, the are committed to make up the difference out of pocket.

Jeanne and I had both made our minimum by Day Zero, but we had some checks which needed to be turned in. ALC had also established some incentives. I met the first by raising $1,000 early on, for which I would be receiving a really nice ALC windbreaker. With the kindness and caring of all of my sponsors, my third self-pledge, and some last minute assistance from Jeanne, I was also able to break the $5,000 mark by Day Zero as well, and for that I received a very special jersey.

Finances now taken care of, we moved over to get our tent assignments. They give you a small poker chip type tag to wear on a chain around your neck, one for your bag, and one for your tent. Jeanne and I would be in tent E 31 for the next week.

Somewhere in there, we had to make a meal plan selection, either carnivore or vegetarian. I'm all for killing animals, so I went with the carnivore selection, and for that received a nifty hot pink band to go with my orange band I had received for seeing the safety video.

Finally, it was time to pick up our schwag. We all received a nice little gift bag with caps and water bottles, and some had socks or other items from sponsors. With some wheeling and dealing and trading, I was able to get water bottles for all my daughters and X Box caps for all their beaus.

We then walked over to pick up my special jersey and my cool ALC windbreaker. So this is it, MY ONE BITCH. This is my one and only complaint! I have been dealing with ALC for months now, under some pretty stressful and difficult circumstances, and they have handled everything wonderfully, nearly perfectly, with the exception of this one thing.

Even though they asked what size jacket I would need several months ago when I earned it, they only had smaller sizes when I went to pick it up. Admittedly, I am gargantuan, but if my size wouldn't be available, they should have let me know what sizes were available back when I earned it, so I wouldn't have been disappointed.

Eh! Nobody's perfect, and my loss was Jeanne's gain. I was glad she could use it, and it was worth it when I saw how happy she was to have it. Besides, if it wasn't for her help, I wouldn't have made my $5,000 goal, for which I received the cool ALC jersey which was at least two sizes too small for me.

The Ride

The big day had finally arrived, although as far as I was concerned, it was still night. We woke at 3:00 AM after having gone to bed after 11:00. My wife, Laurie, helped get my final stuff together. Actually, Laurie got nearly everything together, but more about that later.

We had arranged to pick up Dave Ellison, a fellow rider and resident of nearby Fremont. When Dave climbed in the car, he was wearing the same "deer caught in the headlights" look which I had seen in the mirror earlier that morning.

My daughter Megan had joined us. I was so grateful for this. Megan is always bubbly and energetic, but somehow her hyperactivity calms me, perhaps because she is so entertaining.

The Cow Palace was a mad house with people getting dropped off from every mode of transportation. Perhaps a half mile before we arrived, we could see people walking, pulling their luggage behind them. As we came closer we could see folks disembarking from buses, cabs, cars, and trucks.

Laurie dropped the three of us off and I ran straight for the bathroom. You know how it is when you're nervous. Had I known how things would turn out, I might have relaxed a little bit more…but only a little.

I had a lot invested in this ride, as did every other Rider and Roadie. I had spent dozens of hours shopping for just the right deals, so I could spend hundreds of dollars on everything from tires to helmets. Thus far I had purchased 12 tubes and used all but three. I bought seven jerseys, seven pairs of cycling shorts, and two packages of new socks. I had bought three used bikes and sold one, bought three cycle computers and broken one, and I bought three wheels and had broken one of those as well. I had ridden through two pairs of tires in my training, and had a brand new third pair for the ride. I was on my second helmet, my second trunk, and my second set of brake pads. I purchased one pair of cycling shoes, cleats, and a spare set of cleats, just in case. I bought a rack, a light, a blinky light for the back, a horn, and pinwheels for my helmet. Maybe I could have done without the pinwheels.

I had ridden approximately 3,700 miles to train for this ride. At an average of 12 mph, this means I spent some 1,850 hours training, which translates to almost eight work weeks at forty hours per week.

I had also tapped into the resources of my wife, my kids, my family, my friends, my customers, and nearly everyone I'd come in contact with since October 17th, 2004. Most people had donated generously, but some had pretty much stopped talking to me. With the help of all these generous folks and my road partner Jeanne, we had surpassed my goal of raising $5,000, by the slimmest of margins. By Day Zero, the total was $5000.50.

So all this was going through my mind as I was in the port-a-potty there, and I decided it would be a shame, if after all this generosity and preparation, I spent the next week hiding in an outhouse.

Even after all the planning, Jeanne and I found ourselves relying on the kindness of a fellow rider to tune our bikes at the last minute, and Jeanne had to find a replacement wheel the day before we dropped our bikes off at the Cow Palace. She ran over one of her wheels when she was bringing her bike to our house for last minute preparations. Perhaps she was a little nervous as well.

I saw many of my old riding friends, all cold and excited, and even the veteran riders looked apprehensive. Alan and Stephanie had joined up to form "Team Paradise" and had mini palm trees coming out of the top of their helmets. Shelly had her feathers on her helmet and was gathering with others from the feather contingent. Julie Brown had devil horns on her helmet and Lydia had horns on her bike. They were riding as the evil twins, but Lydia couldn't figure out how to keep her horns on her helmet.

We ran into Kate and Courtney, and the quintuplet contingent. We were finally able to count them all, and even attach names to each of them, Kate, Courtney, Michelle, Ann, and Kim, on the ride.

We also saw Kelly and Tilmin, the Hudson sisters. They ride every year with "Team Pie," and they had cute little slices of pie on their helmets.

There was a lot of excited hugging and "we made its" passed about. Eventually Megan found Jeanne and we all joined up. Jeanne introduced us all to her friend Kay and "pleased to meet yous" were exchanged all around.

Jeanne and I knew we wanted to ride out together, and as it was very crowded, we stuck together...umm... like two people trying to stay together in a large crowd. Opening ceremonies were pretty much non-existent from our perspective. One could tell something was happening, but you didn't know what it was. The sound system could be heard in the front of the room, but not at all in the back. To add insult to injury, they made it up to us later in the week when they played a video tape of the ceremony on the ride, but the slower riders, like Jeanne and I, pulled in too late that evening, and so we missed it again.

Eventually the ride was declared open, and it looked like it would take the whole week just to get all those riders to all those bikes and on the street, but in relatively short order we were all headed in the right direction. We couldn't actually ride for quite a distance, as it was just too crowded.

We walked our bikes through crowds of well-wishers. Laurie had decorated my helmet with pinwheels, and I had brought the extras to hand out. Whenever I saw a tiny kid who looked bored out of his or her mind, and looked horribly sleepy from being dragged out of bed at this ungodly hour on a Sunday morning, I handed them a pinwheel so they could hold a pinwheel…and be bored and sleepy.

I saved the last pinwheel for Laurie, I wanted to give it to her as we said our last tearful goodbye, which was kind of silly, because I was almost certain I would see her, and hopefully some of my offspring in Aptos that evening.

I spotted Megan before Laurie, and she was cheering louder than anyone. I asked Megan where her Mom was, and Meg pointed up the hill. Laurie was cheering and shouting, and generally being as supportive as she had been throughout this entire journey. My biggest concern for the ride all along had been how I would function without her. In our nearly two years of dating and twenty-seven years of marriage, we had spent only a couple of days apart from one another.

We started the ride into a headwind, but we were all traveling at a leisurely pace in a huge pack, taking up the entire right lane of the road. Some of the faster riders even went into the second lane to pass the rest of us. I was happy to see we rode along Lake Merced, which was part of the fateful training ride of '04, and also the Punch and Pie ride which I rode with Megan, and where I rode with Jeanne for the first time. I took that as a good omen.

Just before the first rest stop, we were pushing up a hill when I heard a familiar sweet voice singing "Just what makes that little old ant, think he can move a rubber tree plant?"

It was my first training ride leader, Julie Brown, singing the song she sang to me on my first training ride, and it was wonderful. I couldn't believe I had come this far, but Julie, angel that she is, was here to remind me.

The water stop at mile 21.5 was "manned" by pretty French maids, and I stopped for a picture with one young lady who was directing traffic with a really cute fake French accent.

We picked up the pace and rode at a good clip until we hit highway 92. I had done this ride on a motorcycle, which was difficult enough, but I had never even considered it on a bicycle. I thought Jeanne would be riding ahead of me now, but she had serious problems with her calf cramping, and so I kept right with her.

I was very concerned about making it up this hill, and I was beginning to question what the hell I was doing on this ride at all. The hill was horrid, and the headwind only made it worse. There was no shoulder to speak of, and riders called out "crap road!" as they would otherwise call out "gravel" or "glass" to describe what shoulder there was. While we had done hills this difficult, we had never seen them with so much vehicle traffic, and as such, passing was dangerous. As a slower rider, I felt a great deal of pressure to keep my best pace, so faster riders wouldn't lose patience and risk passing.

Just as everything was falling apart for me, as I was struggling with the monstrous hill and feeling maybe I didn't belong here, I saw a woman holding a yellow sign. I recognized that it made reference to a biblical passage, Matthew 25:36. The sign said simply, "I was sick and you visited me." About then I think I got something in my eye, and it got teary, but I straightened up and rode just a little bit stronger.

Very shortly thereafter, I heard a constant drumming in the distance, and it was almost impossible not to pedal in time to the beat. My pace increased, almost uncontrollably, and before I knew it I could see a group of Taiko drummers at the crest of the hill pounding out a rhythm.

I don't know how, and I don't remember doing it, but I got to the top of this hill before Jeanne. I'm only sure of this because I have a picture of her cresting the hill with our Cat II friend, Jane (I'm right on your tail!). I think that was the last hill I took before Jeanne, excluding some of the little rollers, for the remainder of our journey to LA. We stopped for a bit, and got pictures of diva drag queen and Roadie extraordinaire, Ginger Brewlay, with Jeanne, and then, as with most every stop, we quickly returned to the road.

The rest of the ride to Highway 1 was an easy downhill cruise. It's a ride I've done many times in a car, but it has never been this beautiful! There was so much to see, and so much I'd taken for granted at higher speeds.

Eventually we turned south on Highway 1, and we had an incredible tailwind. I pulled away from Jeanne on the huge rolling hills, but she was always within view. Rest Stop 2 was manned by bands of the eighties, and traffic was directed by two members of the band "Kiss." Jeanne and I regrouped, refueled on Clif bars and drinks, and hit the road.

The rollers continued, and I'm not one to waste momentum. I rode as hard as I could on the downhills, so as to avoid suffering on the uphills. I pulled into lunch, and thought Jeanne was right behind me. I waited...and waited. I knew something was wrong. When she finally arrived she was pretty upset, and still shaking.

Apparently she had had a leg cramp and pulled over to stretch it out. She had unclipped her left foot to stop, but when a rider came by she leaned right to let them by. She started falling over down a hill on the side of the road. She had no way to stop herself as her right foot was still clipped in. She and the bike, still attached to her right foot, rolled down the side of the hill. It must have been quite a picture, Jeanne, then the bike, Jeanne, bike, Jeanne, bike, Jeanne. She said she could see the bike over her as they rolled down the hill. She was thinking, on Day One, the ride was over for her!

Fortunately it didn't come to that. She was scraped and bruised, and we spent most of lunch pulling burrs out of her clothing and skin, but she was able to continue on. The slivers and burrs were a lasting memory though, as Jeanne removed the last sliver four days later. I felt really guilty for not having been with my road partner in her moment of need, but in reality, all I would have been able to do for her was tell the story from a second vantage point. The good news is that Jeanne may hold the record for the longest distance ever fallen due to a Failure to Unclip, or an F.U., as I like to call them (I just decided I like to call them this).

While we were eating lunch we could see our ride would begin again at the bottom of a pretty large hill, and our friend Jane (and what a fine tail...) brought up the fact that on a past ride, a fellow rider had had a heart attack taking this hill. It's funny how people often know just the right thing to say.

I know the prime time for a heart attack is right after a big meal, and starting vigorous exercise without a warm up. I let Jeanne know this would be a very slow hill for me.

We continued to have a tailwind, and while the hills were often big, the tailwind and the momentum from speeding down the previous hill made them quite tolerable. Somewhere in all that speeding we broke new records. We compared cycle computers at Rest Stop 3, and Jeanne had surpassed my previous record, hitting 43 mph. I checked my own computer, and had set a new record. I had hit 49 mph and didn't even know it!

Lunch by the ocean, Day One, with the hill after lunch
(Photo Courtesy of Shelly Ross)

There's something special about riding a bike along the ocean, as opposed to driving. You can see the ocean better from a bike, and it was spectacular that day. The colors were amazing and vibrant. Beyond that though, you could just feel the ocean, and smell it, and taste it. Life doesn't get much better than riding like this, and with a tailwind, no less! I was grateful I had lived to see this day.

I rode by Davenport. My Dad was born in Davenport and I thought about my father, and his family. I was indeed fortunate to be born in this time with so much privilege. Perhaps even one generation back, and certainly two, the technology hadn't existed which would keep me alive after my heart attacks. Even if it had, my family, on either my Mother's or Father's side, were in no financial position to seek medical care of that magnitude.

Before I was able to take myself too seriously though, we rolled into Rest Stop 4. The theme was "Dollywood" and it was "manned" by large-breasted blondes in a country motif. Jeanne hates the song "Islands in the Stream" so I thought I'd antagonize her a bit and sing a few bars. Jeanne rode out before me.

Coming into Santa Cruz, there was an older woman holding a large picture of a young man, who I assumed to be her son. Underneath his photo were the dates of his birth, and death. She stood weeping; holding the picture in one hand, and blowing kisses to us with the other, and thanking us. It's not easy riding a bike with tears streaming down your face.

One jersey I saw advertised the ride as "Millions of emotions, Thousands of cyclists, Hundreds of miles, Seven Days, One goal." I expected the ride to be a mix of emotions, but I had no idea how quickly we'd be shifting gears. One minute I was yucking it up with a cross-dressing Dolly Parton look alike, and the next I was weeping uncontrollably with the mother of an AIDS victim.

As we rode into Santa Cruz I recognized we were on Mission Street, and things began to look familiar. We crossed Bay Street, which I knew would lead to my daughter Katelyn's place at UCSC.

Just a few miles before pulling into camp at Cabrillo College in Aptos, Jeanne decided to have one final F.U. I stopped quickly on a yellow, and I guess Jeanne assumed I would take it, as I normally would. I was being extra cautious, which she didn't expect, so she stopped without unclipping and went down for the sixth time (there's a great joke here, but even I know where to draw the line). At this point it's become so commonplace, I barely looked up, and yet I was still able to feel guilty.

We passed the Ugly Mug, a coffee shop in Soquel, and they had a large sign in front of their wonderful establishment which said "Free Drinks 4 AIDS Riders." I was anxious to get to camp so I didn't stop, but you can bet I'll go out of my way to stop by and make a purchase later. Even though I didn't enjoy a free drink, the sign alone did wonders for our morale, and I doubt any of us will ever forget the gesture.

Me, Erin, Katelyn, Megan, Laurie, and Jeanne at the end of Day One (Photo Courtesy of Larry Rachleff)

We turned into Cabrillo College, and there they were, my whole family, I had been afraid I would pass them without seeing them, but even for the other riders, my family can cheer louder than anyone, and so a half mile before I arrived I knew they were all there. It had only been 84 miles, but it felt like years since I had seen them. Of course I got the loudest cheer, with the possible exception of the last rider in. We took a few pictures, my wife Laurie, my daughters, Katelyn, Megan, and Erin, Erin's beau Larry, his Pop Marshall, and my road partner Jeanne. I couldn't have been happier that every one of my kids made it there! This was finals week for Megan at UC Davis, and for Katelyn at UC Santa Cruz. So I knew this was a real imposition for the two of them. Erin and Larry were always busy on the weekends, so I know they had better things to do, especially with Larry's Dad, Marshall, visiting from Detroit. They can't possibly know how much I appreciated seeing them all there!

Erin gave us fourteen dozen homemade chocolate chip cookies to share around camp. I hugged and kissed all my kiddos, and then said a sad goodbye to my wife. Somehow I felt like I was going away to some kind of prison camp or something. It was much too quick a visit, but I knew I needed to get out of my nasty riding clothes.

I left my family and walked my bike into the great unknown of road camp. I had no idea where to go or what to do, but my road partner Jeanne was a veteran. I was so grateful for her help. First, we were asked to show our rider numbers as we walked in. They inventoried us every night to ensure no one was left on the side of the road along the route.

Next, we parked our bikes in bike parking, and covered our seats with shower caps to keep them from being wet in the morning. Jeanne used Laurie's Grandma's early sixties swim cap, complete with decorative flowers, so her bike would be easy to spot. I think Nana would be glad it had been put to good use. We removed all our bike packs and anything we would need for the night.

Then we located the gear truck that corresponded with the letter on our necklaces. We found our bags and went hunting for our tent spot, E 31. I had heard the tents were close together, only inches apart, but actually, there were no inches separating them.

The tent assembly reminded me of a scene from the movie "An Officer and a Gentleman" in which the officer candidates were given simple tasks to complete while being oxygen deprived. Pitching a tent, particularly lining up the tent poles through the little loops proved no easy task after riding 84 miles. The wind was at least twenty mph. Our legs and hands were shaking. We threw our gear into our tent to hold it down, and then proceeded to raise it.

We grabbed our shower bags and a change of clothing, and then raced off to …wait in line for the shower. We showered in shower trailers, men on one side and women on the other. While the shower stalls are semi-private, the changing area inside the trailer is communal. It's always a great joy for me to expose my hugely overweight body to groups of a dozen people or more, but I somehow managed without dying of embarrassment. After getting dressed, I headed to the line for the sinks, which were outside and set up face to face in two rows of four.

Over each sink, at face level, is a mirror the length of the sink and about nine inches tall. When someone was lined up across from you, doing the same tasks as you, it created the illusion that your face was on someone else's body. This was always a good trade for me, and until I caught on, I was thinking all this riding was having a really positive effect on my body, except maybe for the breasts I was sometimes growing.

I shaved at night to save time in the morning. In fact, we did everything we could with the idea of moving out quickly. We knew we weren't fast, and I really wanted to complete every inch if possible, and now Jeanne was thinking along the same line. A good start would be all important if we were to accomplish this goal.

We then headed back to our tent, dropped off our shower bags, hung up our camp towels and hurried off to…get in line for dinner. If you haven't gathered by now, every activity from bathrooms first thing in the morning to bathrooms last thing at night, involves a line. There's a line for dinner, and lunch, and breakfast, and every drink of water or Gatorade, every snack, and the longest line of all is waiting for one of 844 portable toilets provided for us along the route.

We offered Erin's cookies around, and before we got to the mess tent, half of them were gone. The rest went during dinner and announcements. We got our last thank you for them on Day Seven, when someone remembered us for the great cookies we shared.

Announcements start at 7:00 PM and Jeanne and I arrived a bit late. We got a weather report from a very funny and entertaining man named Scott Moore. All of the speakers, in fact, were very entertaining, and for the week they were much better than television!

I thought I had heard correctly, but tonight it was confirmed, we 1,616 Riders and 400 plus Roadies, and our generous sponsors and supporters, had raised 6.8 million dollars. Jeanne cried, as did many others. Last year's ride had raised 4.9 million dollars.

We dragged ourselves to the bathroom line, and then our tent. On the way there I noticed the soccer nets on the field where our tent city had sprung up had been decorated with brightly colored jerseys and shorts. Riders who had laundered their clothing were using the nets as clotheslines.

I called Laurie and we talked until the neighbors shushed me, as became our routine throughout the week. Laur and I said our "goodnights and I love yous." It reminded me of the days before we were married, and I remembered how we hated to hang up. Then, by the light of my little battery operated mini Coleman lantern, I jotted a few notes for my journal.

The wind howled outside our tent, and the tent walls shook and banged. It was exciting and I felt like I was on a huge adventure. Jeanne and I said goodnight. We could hear snoring all around us. I hate to hear snoring, even though I snore so loud I sometimes wake myself.

I remember hearing Billy the Kid once killed a man just for snoring, and I felt somewhat sympathetic for the kid. That first night I remember thinking, "All this snoring, oh my God! I'll never go to sleep!" Then I remember thinking "All this snoring…I'll never…" That's the last thing I remember…I fell asleep.

Strawberry fields and workers…somewhere near Salinas
(Photo Courtesy of Shelly Ross)

Day Two - Aptos to King City

Waking in the middle of the night to use the restroom is never fun. Its worse when you have to climb out of a tent, put on a fleece and shoes, and hike a tenth or two of a mile, knowing you'll be greeted by a port-a-john. The most difficult part of the journey was putting on shoes. My balance was off, there was just nothing to lean on, and my legs didn't want to function correctly after the day's riding.

The leg dysfunction was a common ailment. I noticed whatever muscles you wear out while riding, are apparently the same as those you use to stop when walking. So you just didn't stop walking as soon as you normally would when you're walking at a good clip. I ran into several things and people, and I noticed a lot of others doing the same.

But getting back to my bathroom journey, my first trip was a solo effort. The path was rough and dark, but I somehow managed. We were lectured many times about port-a-potty etiquette, and the number one rule was not to allow the door to slam shut, waking all the other riders. I was always amused when somebody would let the door slam, because they would invariably catch themselves, wince, and return to the door, open it and close it correctly, you know, like when you slammed the screen door when you were a kid and your Mom would make you go out and come back in "the right way."

There were 1,000 tents, which were all exactly the same, so I had a huge fear I wouldn't be able to find my way back. I picked several landmarks and upon my return I was only off by one row, an error which was easily corrected.

On my second bathroom journey of the night I was joined by Jeanne. I noticed the ground was now soaked, and we found ourselves sinking in the lawn. We leaned on each other several times, and finally ended up walking arm in arm to steady ourselves like a couple of drunks. I couldn't figure out why the field had gone so mushy.

The next morning we learned the sprinkler system had gone off in the middle of the night, and some folks had heroically put garbage cans over the sprinkler heads, which saved many tents from disaster, but caused flooding in places.

Jeanne said she had heard people talking loudly, and yelling, and she thought it very rude. I slept through the whole thing. Several tents were displaced. Some folks ended up sleeping in Medical, and one guy was treated for hypothermia.

I only remember being really cold. I had borrowed my daughter's mummy sleeping bag, unaware they come in different sizes. I couldn't fit entirely into the bag. Originally I thought I'd be warm enough in a t-shirt and sweats, but I woke and put on my fleece again. I usually sleep too warm, but the forty degree temperatures and the tiny sleeping bag solved that problem for me. I never did get warm enough that night.

We had set our alarm for 5:00 AM, and apparently, so did everyone else. It was funny to hear all the alarms going off simultaneously, with hundreds of different tones. Getting ready in the morning was awkward, and it was so cold I had difficulty functioning.

Laurie had spent the whole week before the ride getting my gear ready and packed. She made everything easy to locate by actually making a map of my bag to help me find items. It was still dark when we were getting ready, but with my flashlight I could locate stuff on the little map, and then in my bag. She also made a map for my shower bag.

When I opened the zip lock bag holding my riding clothes for Day Two (everything was so organized) I discovered she had written a little romantic and encouraging card, and put it in with the clothing. That warmed me a bit.

Soon we headed off to brush our teeth and wash our faces, and that done, we returned to our tent, packed our gear, dismantled our tent and dragged all our stuff to the gear truck. Then we grabbed our bike packs and headed off for breakfast. As I've already explained about the lines, I'm not going to get into it again except to say the announcement makers would always remind us that each line was an opportunity to make new friends, and I had some very nice conversations in lines.

Every person I met in line had another story, either about the ride or their reason for riding. I heard dozens of moving accounts. Many folks carried pictures of loved ones lost to AIDS somewhere on their person or bicycle. One girl I met had a picture of her father on her back. He had passed away the previous year.

Every morning we would read our "Rider's Digest" over breakfast. It was a compilation of camp news and such, with a weather report, miles to and between rest and lunch stops, menus for the day's meals and other announcements.

There were constant reminders, in every announcement, and every written communication to drink plenty, and eat. The ALC Mantra was "Eat before you're hungry, drink before you're thirsty." Signs everywhere read "Eat Hydrate Pee…Avoid the I.V." making reference to a failure to urinate as a sign of dehydration, and the intravenous fluids one could expect to enjoy should one reach that point.

Breakfast was always good, usually consisting of eggs, potatoes, sausages or bacon, muffins or tortillas, oatmeal, a variety of cold cereals, yogurt, and fruits. Everything was good except the oatmeal, and I never had cold cereal except the last day, when I wasn't so concerned with nutrition.

After breakfast, we hit the bathroom lines one last time. All of the restrooms had a station by them with individually packaged disinfectant wipes, and sometimes large containers of hand sanitizer. Jeanne and I also had little bottles of Purell hand sanitizer attached to our bike packs, which Laurie had supplied for us.

We headed for our bikes, filled our water and Gatorade bottles, and hit the road. I felt good getting back on the bike. I was concerned we were moving too slowly, about 10 mph, but after the first day I realized it just took us a few minutes to warm up in the morning. We took the first hills slowly, but somewhere on a downhill I hit a bump and my water bottle bounced out.

I stopped and went back to retrieve it, and when I replaced it, I noticed my water bottle cage was broken. This was the second time I had broken a water bottle cage (mental note: refrain from buying cheap water bottle cages). A broken water bottle cage is an annoyance, because it makes a rattling, clanking noise, and your water bottle keeps falling out on bumps.

The broken water bottle cage was the biggest mechanical failure I had on my bike. The rider who tuned my bike, Kyle Rich, had done an excellent job. The bike hummed for the entire ride, I didn't have one missed or ghost shift, and things could not have gone better in that department. The only other equipment failures I had were a broken helmet side view mirror, and a slow leak from a tube.

Very early in the morning, we received the blessing of the tailwinds and our speed picked up considerably as we passed through the strawberry fields. At one point, the workers in the fields cheered us on. It was pretty touching. I was grateful for the wisdom of my parents and grandparents, for if not for their good choices and just plain luck, I might be out working the fields as well.

The fields are a huge bore when you're passing in a car, but when you're cruising at bicycle speed; they're nothing short of art. The parallel rows interconnected by dirt roads, with fields of perpendicular rows in the backdrop were dazzling and kept me entertained for quite a while. I guess I was really tired.

Before too long we were at the legendary fried artichoke stand. I had never tried fried artichokes, but veteran riders had described them as the closest thing to heaven, and so I was interested. Jeanne and I split an order and they were excellent, but not worth riding a bike 115 miles. Maybe that's just me though.

We continued on and on, and at some point those artistic rows became every bit as boring as they are in a car. I've said it before; Jeanne and I are almost as fast as anyone on the flats with a tailwind. Jeanne says it's because we make a wider sail. At any rate, we did a lot of passing, and we were only rarely passed.

It was about this point I discovered the bike computer game. We never thought about how many miles were left in a day, unless it was after the last rest stop. Nobody wants to hear there are only 92 miles left today. Instead we always calculated the distance to the next rest stop, or lunch.

The bike computer game consists of calculating the time it will take until the next rest stop. For demonstration purposes we'll do an easy one. Let's say you had nine miles left until the next rest stop, and let's say you were traveling at 18 mph. Then you have a half hour until the next rest stop.

Of course, more often than not, the calculation was much more complex. Sometimes, if the equation was difficult enough, and you were traveling fast enough, by the time you were done determining minutes to the next rest stop, you could start playing the game all over again!

The rules of the game are simple. Never calculate time when you are riding uphill or into a headwind. Always calculate the time when you are going downhill or with a tailwind so you can get the most optimistic time. Finally, the most important rule of all is, calculated time is worthless and means absolutely nothing. I thought I was losing my mind playing this game, but I soon discovered Jeanne, and many of my fellow riders play as well, though their rules may vary slightly.

Around mile ten we came across our friend Shiv lying on the road with her bike down. She already had several riders around her, including her road partner, Kate. I asked if there was anything I could do to help, but they all said they had it covered. I hoped she wasn't hurt too badly, but she was definitely bleeding, and in pain. While we were at the next rest stop, Shiv arrived by ambulance. She got the biggest cheer when they pulled her out and carted her over to Medical. She looked a lot better than she did lying on the road, and I was happy to see her smile.

She acted embarrassed to receive so much attention, but I was guessing that any woman with hot pink dreadlocks probably doesn't mind being noticed. Though her ankle was badly swollen, and she had scrubbed many body parts, the prognosis was good. Shiv would be out for the day, but likely would ride the next day.

We kept on, and I remember at mile 27 I was feeling like there was no way I would finish the day. At one rather insignificant hill I was feeling exhausted. I was really struggling when I noticed some small plastic eggs along side of the road. We recognized them immediately as gifts left by none other than Chicken Lady, or if you're from southern California, that would be THE Chicken Lady.

Chicken Lady has become a living ALC legend. Word has it that "she," with only one exception, has ridden every AIDS Ride in California. Three of those years, she rode in five AIDS rides.

Chicken Lady rides in a fantastic Chicken helmet, carrying a matching chicken handbag filled with plastic chicken eggs. She deposits the eggs on hills throughout the ride, to motivate other riders. She rides her egg yolk yellow chicken bike, with a custom paint job, and lettering on the side which reads "Poultry in Motion."

We eagerly opened our eggs. Jeanne's had a tiny baby chicken, and mine had Orbit gum, some M&Ms and a "Brush Up." I shared my M&Ms with Jeanne, and afterwards, I felt so much better.

Now I have to admit, the thought of a grown man riding around in a chicken get up and hiding eggs hit me as rather odd before I did the ride. But after having my spirits lifted so much by one tiny egg, Chicken Lady has become a true American Hero to me!

Day Two was filled with exciting things to see, from the belly dancers at Rest Stop 1, to Rest Stop 2, manned by toys like Rubik's Cube and the Care Bears. We saw Kermit the Frog and serenaded him with "Rainbow Connection."

We crossed a bridge over a beautiful stream where two beautiful young ladies were skinny-dipping (there may have been some guys swimming there as well, but I don't remember). Jeanne thought I spent too much time "voyeuring," but I just really needed a rest, and besides, I

171

looked the word up, and there is no way I could see actual sex organs at that distance, try as I might, thank you very much!

Jeanne and the "Secret Service" at Rest Stop 4, Day 2

We saw the Cookie Lady with her Dancing Dunkin' Boys. The Cookie Lady makes home made cookies for all the ALC Riders and dressed in a giant cookie with the words "EAT ME" on her back. Her Dancing Dunkin' Boys looked like two giant dancing glasses of milk.

Somewhere near Salinas many of us burst into a rousing chorus of "Me and Bobby McGee." In Soledad we handed small toys and candy to kids who obviously were expecting us, and waited on the side of the road for high fives and gifts.

Day Two also saw some pretty bumpy roads. I remember at one point hearing Jeanne say what I thought was "my nuts," and I begged her pardon as I thought I had surely misunderstood. She replied that she thought she had actually grown some, only to have them smashed. I could relate, well…to the smashing part anyway.

Finally at Rest Stop 4, we were greeted by roadies dressed as the "Secret Service." Maybe "greeted" isn't the correct word, as they pretty much just stood there blankly behind dark sunglasses and ear pieces in their black suits. Things were very quiet until someone "called in" a fake "bomb scare," but the Secret Service has to take every threat seriously, and so they evacuated the port-a-potties, chasing people out with bullhorns and a great sense of urgency.

I rode in to the finish for Day 2 a bit ahead of Jeanne. I know this because I have a picture of her riding in. We parked our bikes and checked our cycle computers. Today had been a century, 100 miles and change. Any time Jeanne and I ride distance and finish averaging in the 12 mph range, we're happy. When we finish in the elevens we're happy too, because we say "what the heck, it's almost twelve." Today we did one hundred miles in seven hours. Of course Lance would laugh at that, but for us it was an amazing 14.3 mph average.

The Chicken Lady on Day Three

Day Three - King City to Paso Robles

I awoke to the morning of Day Three with a feeling of impending doom. Day Three was the day we were to tackle the infamous hill "Quadbuster." It is almost universally considered by riders to be the worst hill on the AIDS/Lifecycle route. I had read so many analyses of it I could almost describe the agony I would be enjoying, minute by minute.

Logically, I knew I had tackled everything they had thrown at me, and Quadbuster (or "The" Quadbuster, if you're from southern California) is just another hill. I'd been assured by none other than the great ride leader Ben (EFHIM) Armstrong, that we'd done worse hills in the Cat II training series. On the other hand, how many times has Ben told me this was "the last hill?"

This brings me to another point. How do they find so many poker-faced individuals to line a 585 mile route and have them all agree to tell you, straight to your face, "Keep going! This is the last hill!" We riders had begun to refer to this phenomenon as the "ALC conspiracy."

Similarly, there were many folks who would line the route and yell things like "Only three more miles to Rest Stop 1!" Or they might yell "One mile to camp!" I theorized there must be some kind of mathematical equation one could use to take the number of miles well-wishers told us we had left, and determine actual mileage. Incidentally, I also believe this same type of equation could be used to extrapolate a woman's true weight, by applying an equation to the weight which appears on her driver's license.

At any rate, I knew Day Three would be tough. I just didn't know how tough, and what can I say? I'm a worrier. I figured we'd best start the day by checking the air in our tires, and so we waited in yet another line of at least a half hour to get hold of a good floor pump with an accurate gauge. What I didn't know until later was the pump Jeanne had bought for me as a "going on the ride" gift had an excellent gauge on it, and was an incredibly good pump. So this was our first and last pump line.

We started off on a horribly rough road, with potholes and crevices galore. You really had to pick your line carefully. I think Jeanne is a bit more cautious than I, so I was a good 300 feet ahead of her.

Prior to beginning the ride, Jeanne and I had some discussion as to how we would handle the ride, and what our best chances of completing it would be. I had received advice from my bike mentor Shelly, an ALC veteran whom I trust and love. She told me to train with anyone, but "the ride has to be your own."

Jeanne and I had gone around and around about whether we would ride together. We were both trying to be polite. We knew from experience we were both barely finishers, and more than one flat in a day, or any other mechanical problems, could jeopardize our riding what other riders referred to as "Every Fucking Inch," or EFI. This had always been important to me. I didn't train this long and hard to ride "almost all the way to L.A.."

Up until recently though, Jeanne had always told me riding every inch was unimportant and she had nothing to prove to anyone. She had been telling me she would be a good tentmate, because she planned on sagging (sag buses are available for riders who are unable to complete the day's course) each day, and she would set up the tent and pull our gear. While she had done the ride two years before, from what I gather, she had completed only a couple of the shorter days.

Ever since our completion of the century on Day on The Ride, I began to observe a change in her thinking. We talked about not riding with anyone else, because a group of riders bound to stay together can travel only as fast as the slowest rider at any given time. Every rider we added to our group of two only increased the chances of flatting or other mechanical troubles.

There was never any question if we rode with anyone, it would be with each other. Since the first time we rode together to Niles, we've been "road partners." Nothing was ever said or anything, and I don't even know how it happened, it just happened like it was meant to be.

Once we completed Day One of the ride, Jeanne absolutely knew she could complete the entire ride and she was pretty determined to do so. In the end, the only thing to which we would both commit was to "play it by ear" or "see how it goes."

Generally, what ended up happening was Jeanne would pass me and pull away from me on every hill. I'm much more aggressive passing, and on the downhills, so I would catch her there, and if there was another hill in sight I would try to pass her and pull away. She, in turn, would catch me and pass when we reached the next hill.

I had purchased these ridiculous little kid's bicycle horns before the ride, and whenever we had been separated for a period of time, once we got within earshot, whoever of us was approaching from behind would squeeze their horn a couple of times. The front rider would honk back to acknowledge the rear rider's message had been received. It was silly really, but it was always reassuring to hear that obnoxious little horn sounding.

We were very comfortable riding together on the flats, and it really didn't matter who was in front. Drafting (riding closely behind another rider in order to take advantage of their slipstream so as to reduce wind resistance) is prohibited on the ALC ride, and on ALC training rides. But sometimes, when you're really tired and going at a slow pace into a headwind, it just happens. It does make a huge difference in the amount of effort the rear rider has to exert.

We always waited for each other to pull in at rest stops. Occasionally Jeanne would have to wait for me at the top of a hill, and rarely, when I was leading, if I felt we had been out of contact for too long, I would stop and wait for Jeanne.

One such occasion was the morning of Day Three. Verbal communication is quite an effort when you're riding at any speed at all. It always involves quite a bit of yelling and repeating, and more yelling, and often ends with "NEVERMIND!" Usually, it just wasn't that important anyway.

More than once I heard Jeanne yell "RUSS!" I would go through the routine of calling out "SLOWING!" Pull over to the right, let Jeanne catch up to me, have her pass, catch back up to her, begin to pass her and ask "WHAT?" only to have her say something like "Did you see the seagull back there?" I'll admit sometimes it was just easier to smile and nod knowingly, rather than go through that whole scenario. At this point I would like to state for the record, that in my marital relationship, I always pay very close attention, and would never just smile and nod.

So, that morning on Day Three, I was out about 300 feet ahead of Jeanne. I made a right turn and I could see Jeanne out of the corner of my eye, and she yelled "RUSS!" really,

REALLY loud and excitedly, as if it was the first time we'd seen each other on the ride. So I waved. I waved as I might wave to any of my special friends, because frankly, she was yelling her greeting as most of my special friends do, calling my name like one might yell out the window of the short bus.

About this time I passed two young ladies on really cute matching purple Magna mountain bikes. I often notice the bikes folks are riding. You'll see names like "Specialized" or "Trek" or "Cannondale" or "Fuji" on the ride pretty frequently. "Magna"… not so much.

"Magna" is a brand sold at Target Stores. It is a very heavy bike, with no quick release components. I hate to be a bike snob, but I literally could not do the ride on a bike this heavy, with not so good components, because I need every advantage I can get.

Every night at announcements, people told stories they'd heard from the road. One of the stories the previous night was about two sisters who had walked into a fast food restaurant and noticed flyers for two charity fundraising events. They thought they'd like to do something like that. One of the flyers was for ALC, and the other was for Walk for Life.

Upon closer investigation they found the Walk for Life had passed already this year, and so that simply and quickly they decided to do the AIDS/LifeCycle.

Of course they had to be outfitted, so they ran over to Target to get bikes. Honestly they looked like they spent a lot more money on actual outfits than bikes. They were cute as bugs' ears in their shorts (not bike shorts), white jackets, and white tennis shoes. The Target Twins didn't ride every inch, but they rode respectably, and I think their folks should be very proud of them.

While I passed them, I asked if I could take their picture, and they were happy to oblige me. I got a good distance ahead

179

of them, stopped and snapped the picture. About this time I realized that Jeanne should have passed me, but she didn't, and so I knew something was wrong.

I crossed the street and headed back to find her. This was the first time I'd ridden against the grain, and I got a good look at our little stream of humanity. I was pretty choked up. We looked like a little rag tag army in spandex. Folks were wind burnt, sun burnt, taped, bandaged, bruised and scraped. People were shiny with sunscreen, and some had covered lips or noses with zinc oxide, which in many cases had bugs imbedded in it. We were beautiful!

So, about a mile back I found Jeanne changing her tire. She was pretty much done, but I helped her finish up, pump up the tire and put it back on. Some time before Rest Stop 1, someone riding behind us mentioned Jeanne had a bent rim. Sure enough, it looked like it would need some work.

We rode on to Rest Stop 1 where there was a lot of nervous chatter, the likes of which I hadn't seen since the morning of Day One. The line for the bathroom was the longest I had yet seen. Quadbuster was already taking a toll on folks, and we had yet to see it. Even many of the veteran riders looked apprehensive.

Jeanne looked at her rim and found she had two broken spokes. She took her bike to have the bike techs take a look. The news was grim. The technician said he'd do what he could, but he didn't have her size spokes, and she might have to sag to the next rest stop, or lunch, where they had a larger truck, which might have her spokes.

Jeanne was pretty upset. She was riding well, had completed two difficult days and was having no problems taking hills. She was all psyched up for Quadbuster, and she knew she could do it. The thought of having to sag, to not ride EFI, and to skip over the biggest challenge of the ride was really disheartening.

Jeanne and I were "road partners." The term brings up all kinds of romantic notions of famous partners from the past. I thought of Butch and Sundance, and how they came to a point where they only had one horse, and so they had shared it. I looked at Jeanne, and I looked at myself, and I started figuring out how I was going to tell Jeanne "Too bad, so sad! See ya at lunch!"

Fortunately, the bike tech did an amazing thing. He took extra long spokes, and intertwined them with spokes remaining on her wheel, and made the wheel true enough to get her to lunch, or even through the day if need be. I never saw anything like it.

We left Rest Stop 1 to conquer Quadbuster. It's unmistakable when you approach it. All of the mammoth hills we've seen, thus far, twist and turn and you never know what might be around the next corner. With Quadbuster, you see it all right at the beginning, but you wish to God you hadn't.

I took a gander and I don't think I ever even glanced up to the top again. I literally just put my head down and went to work. Almost as soon as I'd begun the climb, Robert, a man whom I'd briefly met on Day on The Ride was standing at the side of the road trying to take pictures. He was asking if anyone might have any AA batteries for his camera.

I'd been on this ride now for three days, and I'd already learned in this little Utopian society of ours, you can't say "no" if someone needs help. It would just be unthinkable. We were all here to make this journey as perfect as possible for each other, and not once had I asked anybody for anything and been turned down.

On the other hand, I had made a vow to God and myself, that unless my body failed me, I would ride every hill without resting, and ride every inch of the way. So I told Robert I couldn't stop, but I had batteries in my bike trunk in a camera case. If he could unzip the trunk, he could take the whole case, take the batteries, and if we happened to run across each other later, he could return the case.

So Robert jogged behind me and pulled the case, and I continued on at my slowest pace.

I remember there was a turn-out, and it was packed with folks catching their breath. I plodded on. I passed a few people who were walking. One of them was in tears. I tried to comfort her in the short time we traveled together. I told her she was an amazing walker, and that I had trouble catching up to her, and I was riding! She managed a smile as I passed.

Many riders passed me. Some were faster than others. Some had reassuring words for me. "You're almost there." "You're gonna make it!" Two riders who passed me were crying, and I thought "Sheesh! Why are you crying, you're passing me!" Some would ask how I was doing.

I remember someone, a fellow rider, had stopped and was pounding a rhythm on a guardrail with some kind of stick or something, and you know, we Hispanics like that rhythm. I picked up the pace for a bit, but only for a bit, and then I was almost out of breath.

I slowed again, back to my 2.9 mph pace, and caught my breath. I was sweating profusely. I had removed my sunglasses as they were all full of sweat and I couldn't see out of them anyway. I had unzipped the zipper on my jersey as far as it would go, in that ever-so-cool look. Jeanne said I looked like Tony Soprano, with a plastic whistle instead of gold "bling."

Many women who have done both, say the ride is like childbirth, and I imagine that's particularly true of Quadbuster. Looking back, it seems like it wasn't that bad. Before long I was approaching the top and there were all the smiling faces. Whenever I saw folks cheering, it always made things easier, and there were never more folks cheering us on than at the peak of that infamous hill.

Mom and Dad were there. Not my Mom and Dad, but an older couple who manage to find their way to the top of every hill to root for us and give us cookies and snacks. All the riders call them "Mom and Dad." They made it here against the odds too. They were involved in a car accident on their way from Ventura, but that didn't deter them from coming. There were at least fifty riders who had pulled over to cheer on fellow riders. There was also our cheerleader rider who played music from her iPod through a little megaphone, danced, and cheered us on. My friend Jeanne was also there at the top, cheering as loud for me as anyone.

So Quadbuster (or "The" Quadbuster if you're from Southern CA), was only 1.3 miles long, and took me about 24 minutes. For my fellow statistic geeks, I've already done the math. That's an average blazing speed of 3.25 mph. That's also 24 minutes of me pushing and pulling with my legs as hard as I could. The name "Quadbuster" certainly suits it. I was really happy Jeanne and I didn't have to do this on one bike!

Well after the ride was over, Tilmin Hudson told us her version of her ascent up Quadbuster. She swears she can stay upright at 1.8 mph, so she must be quite a vision, wobbling all over the road. She says three different people helped push her up the monstrous hill, each taking a different section. She summed it up saying "It takes a village to get me up Quadbuster!"

We rode a nice downhill to Rest Stop 2, and then to the little town of Bradley. The School in Bradley does a barbecue fundraiser, serving the riders good food, and raking in a fairly good chunk of money for their school. Jeanne and I were too late to enjoy the barbecue. We were too slow, and so they had sold out. We had to settle for the ALC standard issue sandwiches.

While the food was generally really good during the other meals, lunch was getting pretty bland, and repetitive, and this was a huge disappointment. Still, at this point, we could have eaten the cardboard we sat on to avoid getting burrs in our bottoms.

Shade was scarce here, and it was pretty hot and dry. We all squeezed into whatever shade was available. While we ate, kids from the little community sold pens to raise funds for the school, and I bought quite a few.

That afternoon we spent a good deal of time riding on 101 (or "THE" 101 if...) and it was hard to find a good line. The further to the right you rode the worse the debris and bumps in the road. The best line was just to the right side of the white line just adjacent to the right lane of the freeway. But nobody wants to rub elbows with traffic going seventy miles an hour. On the other hand, we were talking some serious slipstream here!

Perhaps the highlight of the day was Rest Stop 4. As soon as I pulled in, I bumped into Shelly, who told me no matter what, I shouldn't miss "the show." The theme for Rest Stop 4 was the Sound of Music. We went to a small area where we waited. There were about 10 chairs facing one direction. The Quintuplet Contingent was there, and we briefly argued over who would sit in the chairs. The Quints were respectful of their elders, and I respected young ladies. In the end they won, not only the chair argument, but a place in my heart forever.

I sat in an actual chair, a very rare commodity at rest stops, while the Roadies performed for us as the Von Trapp Family Singers. They sang a hilarious version of the Do Re Mi song, and performed a nice little X rated puppet show. What a break it was to laugh so uncontrollably after riding so hard!

RS4 was located at Mission San Miguel, and after the show Jeanne and I did a bit of shopping. I bought some gifts for my wife and daughters, and then we hit the road again.

We rode about a tenth of a mile and made a left turn up a horrible hill; it was brief, but probably the steepest climb we've ever done. Quite a few riders walked it, and some who rode it fell over sideways. I was concerned I might not make it, but I refused to clip out, so failure was not an option. If I couldn't do it, I was in for one of those embarrassing and painful zero velocity accidents. That was all the motivation I needed.

We finally completed the day's route, and we were pretty exhausted. It was 75.8 miles. I remember as we rode out that morning, they were sending us on our way with calls of "Short day today," and I was thinking "YES! We only ride 75.8 miles today!" And then I thought, "What in the hell have I done to myself that I'm all excited about riding *ONLY* 75.8 Miles?!" It was not an easy day.

The announcements were great on Night Three. We were given a rousing talk by Anna Heath, who is a board member of the Positive Pedalers. She was an elegant speaker, and she hit me as the kind of lady I could be good friends with. She really touched us. It was pretty heart warming to see 1600 plus dead tired riders rise to their feet as she spoke. You know that was one sincere standing ovation!

The night ended with a comical Roadie fashion show…but I was so tired I don't really recall much of it. As I was drifting off to sleep, I remembered earlier that morning, a sore and exhausted female rider saying, "Next year I'm going bowling for AIDS."

I slept very well.

185

"The Von Trapp family singers" at Rest Stop 4, Day Three
(Photo Courtesy of Shelly Ross)

Me…pretty self-explanatory
(Photo Courtesy of the guy behind me in line)

Day Four - Paso Robles to Santa Maria

Day Four was set to be our second century of the week. As I'm writing this, it seems ludicrous. I worked just shy of a year to prepare for the first and only century I'd ever done. There I was doing my second and third century with only a day separating them, and the day between was over 75 miles with a hill called Quadbuster.

We were not only scheduled to do 100 miles, but we also had some serious hills to climb on day four. Today we would battle the hills known as "The Evil Twins." My friend and mentor, Shelly, had told me that last year she was halfway up the first of the twins before she realized she was on it. My experience was a bit different.

Exhaustion was beginning to take its toll on most of the group now. I remember being in the breakfast line and staring into space, and into the space I was staring walked a young man, probably not twenty years old, warming his hands on a cup of hot chocolate. The steam from the cup surrounded his face, as he stared bleary eyed into space, just as I was doing.

I wondered what his story was, and why he was here, and I wondered if he had been through as much I went through to get here. And I thought probably so, and the fact that I was here at all was a near miracle. I had survived a couple of heart attacks. I had to get all that gear and do all that training and all that fundraising, and it really was a miracle that everything had fallen into place as it did.

And then I got to thinking, everybody has their crap they have to overcome. Maybe they didn't survive a heart attack, but many folks have survived something else. Maybe they aren't old and overweight, but maybe they're terrified to ask for donations, and fundraising is their big hurdle. And I looked at that young man and guessed it was probably a miracle he was here too. Through him, I could see it was probably a miracle that any of us were here, but that more than 2,000 of us could be here to do this ride was certainly and truly a huge miracle!

About this time I noticed the young man was now glancing back at me from the corner of his eye, squirming uncomfortably and shifting his weight nervously from side to side. I looked anywhere but in his direction. Exhaustion was beginning to take its toll.

The ride out of King City was beautiful, but before too long we were getting into the hills, and they seemed endless today. Today, more than any day on the ride, I struggled with them. Usually my legs keep me from going any faster up a hill. Today, it was my heart which was hitting its limit.

It's been seven years since I had my second heart attack, and I'm not interested in going for a third. I'm not even sure whether putting physical stress on my heart could lead to a heart attack, but I'm not a big gambler, and I don't see any point in testing it to find out. Some people say doing the ride takes a heroic effort, but I'm no hero. I don't mind working hard for a good cause, or even struggling and suffering, but if I can avoid it, I'd rather not die for this, or any other cause.

As soon as I felt any twinge, or even a hint of pain in my heart, I slowed down until I felt perfect again. I was fully prepared to stop if slowing didn't make my heart stop bothering me, but it was never necessary. Still, I was slower than my normal slow.

Apparently, Shelly had become a part of the "ALC conspiracy." The Evil Twins turned out to be the most difficult portion of the ride for me. Let me just say whoever named the Evil Twins will never make it as an accountant. There aren't just two hills, but rather, a whole series of hills. Eventually, though, I made it to the peak, and when we got there, we were at the highest point of the ride.

We stopped for pictures under the elevation sign. There was a bit of a line, but that was nothing compared to the line we saw when we reached the halfway point of the ride.

There's a turn off in the road and large boulders overlooking Morro Bay. Ginger Brewlay had made a sign for previous year's riders which said "Half the way to LA" and there was some controversy as to the grammar. But I just figure Ginger's a So Cal gal. This year she made an additional sign which said (correctly) "Halfway to LA."

As Nor Cal riders, we got in the wrong line. I had seen photos of many past riders with this particular sign, holding their bikes over their heads victoriously, and having my photo taken here would be the fulfillment of a dream. This was a huge landmark for me, a huge accomplishment in and of itself, and no matter what happened from here on out, I would always be able to say I had ridden my bike half way from San Francisco to Los Angeles, and have the picture to prove it!

So we waited in line for well over an hour to climb up on this rock and get our picture taken. While I was waiting I noticed everyone would wait until they were supposed to climb up on the rock to instruct the person behind them on how to use their camera. Some people waited until they were actually on the rock to make wardrobe changes. I hope nobody thought I was too pushy, but I left my bike with Jeanne, walked to the front of the line, and began directing everyone to speed things up. I helped everybody get on the rock, and then lifted their bikes up to them. Just a side note here, those carbon fiber bikes are incredibly light.

While I was helping folks up on the rock, I helped a gentleman up who had a picture on his back I had seen before. For fundraising purposes I had made business cards with the ALC logo on them, and I had received the artwork to make them from a rider from Washington, DC, named Lloyd Carrera. As I do with most ALC folks I "meet" on the Internet, I looked him up on his ALC homepage. Where most riders have a picture of themselves on their page, Lloyd has a picture of his brother, Larry, who lost his battle with AIDS.

Lloyd and I had written a few times to one another, and he was one of the people I was really hoping to meet along the road. I introduced myself, and he hugged me like I was family he hadn't seen in years. We were both hurried, but it was a real joy to meet him. We ran into each other many times after this first meeting.

So while we were waiting for our turn, and I was helping everyone along, a Roadie official was calling out "The caboose is thirty minutes away, and when it arrives you will either have to ride out from here, or be sagged to the next rest stop." It appeared I was going to have to make a choice between riding EFI, and getting my picture taken here.

We heard the twenty minute warning and still had a ways to go. At the ten minute call I began to lose hope, but by the time they called five minutes we were almost there. Our turn came and I dashed up on the rock. I had my picture taken twice just to be sure. Then I pulled Jeanne up and we took one together. I jumped down and was about to pull my bike down and put hers up for her picture, but Jeanne said she didn't care which bike it was, and to save time she had her picture taken with my bike.

As Jeanne climbed down we heard the Roadie call "The caboose is three minutes behind you!" We jumped on our bikes and were on our way down the hill, which was rumored to be a six mile downhill. That helped us out considerably, but the race with the caboose was on.

Jeanne and I had learned early in our training that to keep up, we had to keep going, and where faster riders had the luxury of socializing or actually resting at rest stops, we were in and out as quickly as possible. There was no lounging for us! People ask me how often we rested on the ride, and when I tell them about rest stops, they always seem to have this picture of us pulling up at a rest stop, sitting at a picnic table, drinking a Heineken, and chatting about the weather.

In reality though, thus far we had actually only sat at one rest stop on Day One, where I pulled up a nice cushy piece of asphalt and actually laid and stretched. We also sat to watch the Von Trapp Family Singers at Rest Stop 4 on Day Three. Other than that we never sat, and really never rested. We stood in lines for restrooms, Clif bars, water and Gatorade.

One day, as we were lined up for Gatorade at a rest stop, I asked those at the front of the line, "What flavor is it?" An exhausted female rider turned and replied grimly, "It really doesn't matter…none of it tastes like beer."

If only one of us had to use the bathroom, the other would refill bottles and pick up food. By Day Four though, we found consistent application of butt butter was crucial, so we both used the bathrooms at most rest stops.

We were among the most modest of riders and always applied butt butter in the port-a-potties. ALC was providing small, individual sized tubes at every rest stop. Butt butter is applied where your body meets the bike seat, and provides some relief where your skin is burning. It is mainly intended to lubricate your skin against the padding in your bike shorts. By now, many riders were simply reaching into their shorts and applying publicly.

Day Four also brought us Scott the cheerleader, a very friendly man dressed in a rather conservative skirt, and holding pom-poms. We'd seen Scott throughout the ride, singing old songs with new lyrics he's made up about the ride. Today he was straddling a huge painted line going across the road. He'd shift his weight to the northern side of the line, pointing with his pom- poms, and then shift back over to the southern side and point that way, all the while repeating "Northern California!...Southern California!" He was letting us know our hard work had now taken us across the line into Southern California and we welcomed the news.

We always made a point of taking a leisurely twenty minutes or more for lunch, and even though we were pressed for time, Day Four was no exception. We ate lunch with our buddy Kurt from the CAT II training rides. His quick wit and great sense of humor made the whole ride experience better for all of us, and as we ate, I let him know it.

Kurt's response really made me think. He said that when you're small in stature, and when you're gay and you come out in Junior High School, being funny helps limit the number of beatings you take. I've had my ass kicked while being called a "faggot" in Junior High, and I don't imagine actually being gay makes it any easier to take. I'd like to think things are better now than they were when I was a kid, but I worry that they're not.

On Day Four I sent a post card to Laurie from the Water Witch water stop. I was missing her and our home and family so much, I told her I'd even be happy to watch home decorating shows with her. I scribbled it quickly, as the race with the caboose was still on. The Pismo Beach Chamber of Commerce kindly provided cards and postage. Oh, and by the way, the prettiest picture I took from the whole ride was of Pismo Beach.

I remember quite a few "surprise" hills toward the end of Day Four, the worst of which Riders dubbed "Pismo Bitch." I was passing one very young lady going up this hill. She appeared to be very athletic and strong, so if I was passing her, I knew she was probably having some serious physical problems. She was struggling, and she asked how much further. I think we were well over eight miles from the next stop, and I became part of the ALC conspiracy and lied and told her we were less than six miles out. She told me she wouldn't make it. I told her I was old and fat, and I had a bad heart, and I was going to make it, and that she was young and strong and perfect, and she was certainly going to make it!

I wish I had stayed with her and encouraged her, but the truth was, while I was fairly confident, I had my own doubts about whether I'd get there, and I thought it might be pretty discouraging for her if I had a heart attack and dropped dead after that little speech of mine. So I rode on, continuing our race with the caboose.

We saw a new twist on the ALC Mantra today. One sign had the standard "Eat before you're hungry...drink before you're thirsty" but then added "...Pee before you pee your pants." Were we that exhausted?

I wish I had known just after these hills we'd have great tailwinds, which of course we desperately needed. I remember playing the bike computer game often! The route closes each day at 7:00 pm. We pulled in at 6:40. We were completely drained! We went to grab our gear and tent from the gear trucks, but one of the gear truck guys told us our tent was already at our site, and I understood him to say our gear was there as well. We scouted out our site and found only our tent. We were so tired after riding 100 miles, this was just heartbreaking. So we summoned up our last bit of nothing, and dragged ourselves back to the truck again to find out where our bags were. Our gear truck lady told us our gear was stacked at the corresponding letter of our gear truck, which was used to mark our tent area.

Of course the letter markers were on the opposite side of the tents from the gear trucks. For three days now they had trained us to pull our gear a certain way, and now, for no apparent reason, they were changing the rules of the game, adding perhaps a quarter mile of walking to our day. I was upset. Jeanne was livid! She fired the only harsh words I had heard to or from anyone on the ride.

I felt exactly like Jeanne, I just didn't say anything. Tears were welling in her eyes as she told the Roadie that it didn't really help us to put our gear in a different location after they had programmed us (Jeanne's words) to pick up our stuff from the truck. It was an unfortunate occurrence.

Jeanne knew, just as well as I, that the lady she was upset with was a volunteer saint, like every other Roadie. She knew somehow they had done this to help us out, in some way we just couldn't see. In all likelihood this poor angel of a woman had nothing to do with the decision to move the bags. It seems like such a small thing to get worked up about, but we were just that exhausted.

The ride had broken us down to this point, and this was definitely the lowest point of our seven days. We were beat, sore, blistered, bruised, and bleeding. Jeanne was still pulling slivers out of her body, and was recovering from some stinging road rash from her crash on Day One. We were hurting, and we were looking for somebody to blame. The gear truck lady, kind soul that she was, just drew the lucky number. Jeanne felt awful afterwards, but it wasn't as if she hit the lady, or called her mother names, or even cursed her. Gear truck lady, if you're out there, please understand…and we're sorry. We dragged ourselves to our gear, grabbed our stuff, pitched our tent, and headed for the showers just in time to see the last rider pull in. It was really wonderful to see our friend Kelly had completed the century, and that quickly, in the span of less than twenty minutes, we went from the deepest depths of one of the worst depressions I've ever known, to pure elation! We cheered and hooted wildly and yelled for Kelly like we had just won the lottery, and we wouldn't have been any happier if we had!

Kelly is a pretty resolute woman. She's told us stories of past rides and skipping rest stops to avoid being sagged because she was one of the last on the route. Tilmin told us that one day Kelly was overheated and thought she'd go to medical to get a little ice. Medical immediately took her temperature, and pulled her bike so she couldn't continue. Kelly was running a fever of 104.

We had been panicked when, at one point during the day, we were three minutes ahead of the caboose, the last truck. Kelly later told us about the pressure of her day as she spent much of the time watching the caboose in her rearview mirror. She said she skipped the last rest stop, because she thought they would probably sag her, and she was determined to continue. Riding by the rest stop put her ahead of maybe eight riders, but when she had gone more than 25 miles with nothing to eat, somebody stopped her to insist she do a Gu shot, and she knew she'd never be able to finish without eating something. That was enough to put her back just ahead of the caboose.

The route is supposed to close at 7:00 PM. Jeanne and I pulled into camp at 6:40, and went through the whole gear truck fiasco. We were dead on our feet and moving at the speed of a herd of turtles, so it had to be well after 7:00 when Kelly rolled in.

I have never seen such a look of determination in my life. Kelly was clearly in pain, exhausted, crying, and yet at the same time we could tell she was elated at her accomplishment! She appeared almost shocked, as if she didn't believe she was finishing.

Later, Kelly told us she felt like she'd won the Olympics with all the cheering. How could she not cry? It was one of the most inspirational moments of my life. I only wish I could have been at the very end of her Day Four. I've seen pictures, and Kelly was clearly overcome with emotion upon the completion of that ride.

The last rider ritual says as much about the ride as anything else. Throughout the day, about twenty motorcycle riders who make up our moto-crew, assist us by directing us through intersections and warning us of hazards, all the while doing some pretty serious encouraging and cheering. As the last rider rolls by, moto-crew riders fall in behind them, so by the time the last rider rolls into camp, they have a whole contingent of motorcycles escorting them. Meanwhile, back at camp, an announcement is made letting folks know the last rider is approaching. Many people drop what they are doing and run over to cheer the rider. There is no doubt the last rider of the day is the most revered! As one rider told me, "we're not all safely home until the last rider rolls in." Oh yeah! Kelly told us the last rider also gets a coupon good for a one hour massage!

After Kelly rode by, we showered, and then went for dinner. We turned in early, and we were completely spent. Tomorrow would be the shortest day of the ride, and we desperately needed it.

Gear trucks with gear laid out as it's supposed to be!
(Photo Courtesy of Shelly Ross)

The tent city the morning of Red Dress Day
(Photo Courtesy of Bob Katz)

Day Five - Santa Maria to Lompoc

Today we woke at our usual time, 5:00 AM, but we allowed ourselves to hit the snooze alarm twice and lounge for a while. This would be our shortest day, 42 miles and change. We knew it would be a breeze, and for the first time in five days, we found time to relax.

I don't know what I expected of the ride. I knew it would be difficult, and grueling, and exhausting, but I had no idea we would constantly be moving at such a frantic pace.

I laugh now when I think about my plans for the ride. I brought playing cards and Jeanne brought board games. I had these fantasies of us sitting at picnic tables with other riders playing poker, or Jeanne and I back in our tent lying on top of our sleeping bags saying "Gin!"

In reality the alarm went off each day at 5:00 AM. I'm not exaggerating when I say by 5:01 AM I was stuffing my sleeping bag into the stuff sack. I found if I got this step out of the way, the tent was less cluttered and all the other steps went faster. I undid the valves on my mattress, let the air out, and rolled it up. I turned my back to Jeanne, read my daily note from Laurie, and then pulled out my clothes for the day. I stuffed yesterday's riding clothes in today's bag, and stuffed that into my gear bag. Then I got dressed, with my back to Jeanne, and I assume she had her back to me as well, although for all I know she was spying on me the whole time.

We stood in line for the bathroom, hit the sink line, brushed teeth, washed faces, and combed hair. Then, we determined whether it would be faster and more efficient to go straight to breakfast from there, carrying what I called our hygiene bags with us (Jeanne called hers her HyRuss bag), or should we take our gear and tent to the truck first, then grab our bike packs and carry them to breakfast. This all depended on the layout of the camp, and yes, we were that concerned with conserving our energy.

I think it's worth noting that both Jeanne and I kept all our money in our bike packs, and while we took our gear bags and tent to the truck, or when we picked them up from the trucks, we would just leave our bike packs in the little space which was designated for our tent. We knew our space would be respected, and if anybody took them, it would only be to turn them in to lost and found.

The level of trust and caring among fellow riders was something which I have only experienced in the confines of my own family. Anybody you saw or met would help you with anything that you asked. If you lost something, you knew it would be in the lost and found at the end of the day. Jeanne counted on this some days. She would ride out in her heaviest jacket on the coldest mornings, knowing she had no place to pack it. As soon as the day warmed up, Jeanne would pull into the first rest stop and tell them she had found the jacket. Then, at the end of the day, she would pick it up at lost and found.

We ate breakfast at a calm pace every day, but as soon as we were done eating, we were off for the day's riding. Rest stops were always hurried. Lunch was usually about 20 minutes, and while we talked during meals, again, as soon as we were finished eating we were off.

After our day's ride we continued this pace while pulling our gear, pitching our tent, showering, and brushing our teeth. Sometimes we made it to dinner before the 7:00 pm announcements were made, but just as often we didn't. We ate our dinner, listened to whatever announcements might be left, and when we were done eating, if there were no more announcements, we headed to pick up Internet messages if it was still light out. If it was dark, we headed straight for our tent to call Laurie, jot down some notes, and sleep.

Up until Day Five, this had been our life. We were some of the slowest riders of those finishing, with (I'm guessing) somewhere between 80% and 95% of riders finishing before us. For many of these faster riders it was a completely different world. Jeanne had spoken to the guy who tuned our bikes up before the ride. Kyle told her on Day One, he had finished riding at 11:00 am.

Faster riders also had perks which we never saw. If you rode in early enough, you could make a reservation for a massage. The closest we ever came to a massage was once when I tried to work a kink out of Jeanne's thigh with my forearm, but even with the tent all the way opened, I stopped because it just sounded too weird with her moaning "Oh my God! That hurts! Keep Going!"

One day a family who owned a pizza parlor brought in tons of pizza for the riders. Apparently all the faster riders went to Jeanne's school of Lasagna etiquette (see Training Ride Journal -Petaluma and Beyond!), because all Jeanne and I ever saw were the empty pizza boxes. We did however, enjoy the smell, and in fact our first post-ride meal was pizza.

So Day Five, with only 42 miles, was very special for us. It was even more special for me, because after hitting the snooze alarm twice, it was now almost daylight, and when I was reading

Laurie's daily card, I made a discovery! Every morning thus far, in the dark of the morning, I was able to read the message she wrote inside her cards. The dark ink showed nicely against the white background. But in the light this morning, I noticed she had also written on the front of the card, which had a colored background.

I went back through the past cards, and sure enough, she had put a little inspirational quote or poem on each card. It was wonderful going back and reading them all! It hardly seems necessary to state the obvious, but Laurie was unbelievably supportive in this endeavor from start to finish!

Day Five was also "Red Dress Day." ALC lore has it this day originally started out as "Dress In Red Day." Riders thought it might be nice to create a giant red ribbon along the road if everyone wore red. But folks being who they are…okay, maybe it's only these folks, the day evolved into "Red Dress Day."

Jeanne and I aren't all that flamboyant, and so we participated in our own little way with red jerseys. There were a few other sticks in the mud. Some folks didn't even wear red jerseys.

Jeanne says she'll wear a red dress next year, but I'm not so sure for myself. The ride has really changed me, and I've grown a lot, but it may take more than a ride and another year to get me in a red dress on a bicycle.

The mood had swung radically from yesterday's mood of exhaustion and dread. You can't look at more than 1,000 folks in red dresses and not smile. Not only that, but everyone was celebrating the short day. 42 miles was miniscule, and the route was scheduled to close at 3:00.

We eagerly began making plans for our free time. Ben Armstrong, Training Ride Leader extraordinaire, had scheduled a team photo of all the Cat II series riders who trained every Sunday together. That was set for 3:30, and it would be good to reunite with all those folks again.

Camp was really something to see. Everywhere you looked there was every imaginable red outfit; red thongs over bike shorts, red mini skirts, red lingerie, red polka dots, red moo moos, red bras, red evening gowns, red gowns with bustles and one guy wearing a giant red ribbon on his back. My personal favorite was the red flamenco dress with matching veil.

I was particularly impressed by the matching skirts, headgear, and jerseys of one team. "Team Martini" had huge martinis on the front of their jerseys, complete with olives. On the back of the jersey it read "Team Martini...the drinking team with a cycling problem!" They had matching red skirts with white ruffles.

I took a lot of pictures on Day Five. Jane (and what a fine tail it is!) wore a sexy red teddy...over black furry riding shorts, a black leotard, and black knee warmers. George Harrison wore a very cute polka dot Minnie Mouse looking dress.

Shelly wore a saucy backless number, with red arm warmers and, of course, red feathers covering her helmet. Many of her friends wore the exact same dress. Of course two people in the same dress at the same event would be a fashion disaster anywhere else but "The Ride." Not one of the men wearing her dress seemed the least bit upset.

Tilmin wore a red blouse, a red glittery skirt, and red shoe covers with red glitter which made me think of the ruby slippers from Oz.

Before we rode out we were handed letters from school children, thanking us for riding. Jeanne's letter advised her to drink plenty of water and she cried yet again.

We started out at a leisurely pace. It was great fun to watch the people staring at all the red dressed riders as we rode out of the town of Santa Maria. I remember a group of landscapers who were particularly amused. We stopped in front of them at a light, and I looked over and waved. They waved back, and I was thinking, as hard as the ride was, it was way more fun than working.

I rode briefly with two guys in red tutus, and I told them they wouldn't last five minutes in those red tutus in my neighborhood. They looked concerned, until I told them they would certainly be attacked...by the gang members who wear the blue tutus.

More than the usual number of cars waved and honked support. Sometimes we got some pretty mean stares, but I dogged them right back, feeling especially macho in my pinwheel decorated helmet. Yes, I might have been clad in pinwheels, but I was one of the few guys riding without a dress today.

We rode out of town just as local kids were walking to school. As we stopped at one light, a young boy about eleven years old crossed in front of us. The guy in the red lace flamenco dress with matching red lace Spanish veil happened to be at the front of the line. The kid walked by, and barely glancing up with a deadpan expression casually commented "Nice dress." It was priceless, and we went into hysterics. He barely noticed, if at all, and walked over and joined his buddies, who were waiting for him on our side of the street.

There were only two rest stops that day. We rode through strawberry fields to the first, and it was the nicest we'd seen in a while, with lush green lawns to lay on. I lay on my back and raised my legs, and watched the folks in red. Rest Stop 2 was in the little town of Casmalia. Just like Bradley, these folks had seen us before, and greeted us warmly. The kids from the local school were dressed in oversized ALC shirts, and many of the riders had gifts of bracelets, small toys, beads or candy. One storeowner in town had placed very large speakers outside of his store, and they were blaring disco tunes. A large group of riders stopped and danced in the street, and we stopped for a bit to watch them.

Dancing in the street in Casmalia

When we started up again, it was straight to the hills, and the early afternoon was filled with them. It was a twenty-one mile stretch to camp, and we were tired from the week's rides, but we knew the reward would be an early end, and an afternoon of fun-filled activities!

On the evening of Day Three, Lorri Jean, Chief Executive Officer of the Los Angeles Gay and Lesbian Center, was giving highlights of the ride, as she had done on a daily basis. She is a great storyteller and was always quite witty. She gave her perspective as a long time observer, but a first time rider. Lorri reported that earlier that day, near the peak of Quadbuster, four women were standing and encouraging fellow riders, by saying "You made it up Quadbuster! Here's a preview of the Evil Twins!" At which point they all lifted their shirts exposing "eight of the most beautiful breasts in California." Jeanne said she saw this, but I wasn't there, as I'm fairly certain I'd remember it.

On Day Five, however, I was struggling up the biggest hill of the day when a very pretty young lady, shouting words of encouragement, treated my eyes to a pair of delightful distractions. I forgot all about the hill, and I was touched at such a silly act of selflessness. I couldn't help but smile. Everywhere we had been, all along the route, people had offered us water or fruit, cookies, licorice, M&Ms, or a friendly cheer, and it always made me ride just a little bit stronger. The flashing young lady had the same effect, except I probably smiled for a bit longer.

I was still smiling as we rode into camp. Roadies had established a second bike parking area, with a sign saying if you wanted to ride into town, you could park there, as if I would ride anywhere for fun, after riding 400 miles over the last five days. I didn't know what exciting activities we'd participate in that afternoon, but I knew they wouldn't involve riding a bicycle!

Lunch was set for the return to camp, which was much later than normal for us. We had really taken our time riding, knowing it was a short day, and now we were famished. I don't want to say that Jeanne gets mean when she's hungry, but that's because I'm afraid of what she'll do to me if she happens to read this before she's eaten.

Jeanne wanted to eat as soon as we rode in. I wanted to pull our gear, pitch our tent, and be showered and actually clean for our CAT II group picture at 3:30. We had both been pretty polite up until this point in our relationship. Now, neither of us seemed willing to give an inch. Jeanne left for the restroom while I went and pulled gear, and when she returned we decided to be friends and compromise. I'd set up the tent, and she'd go get both our lunches. We'd eat at the tent, and then go shower and be ready for our photo.

While I was pitching the tent alone, Kate, of the Shiv and Kate team, came over to help me. I told her I was fine, but she wouldn't take no for an answer. I always liked Kate, and now I loved her! We had the tent up before Jeanne returned, and Kate stayed and watched us eat for a while. She had been in camp since 11:30, and was already rested.

We ate faster than usual and then hit the showers. The line was longer than normal because everyone pulled in within a relatively short period of time. In spite of having to show my not-so-gorgeous body to the other guys, showers had gone smoothly up to now. On Day Five though, I made a pretty embarrassing mistake. I left my clean clothes outside of the shower truck. There I was, naked in a shower changing room, with a bunch of meticulously fit young gay guys, with no clothes. I believe I've had this nightmare before.

Talk about a nightmare! What about all those poor gay guys having to look at my overweight naked body!? The thought gives new meaning to the term "scared straight." By the way, I've made this same kind of joke twice in public, and George Harrison was there both times. I worry he thinks I actually believe ones sexual orientation can be so easily swayed...For the record...I believe we are what we are.

Anyway, when I explained my predicament to my fellow shower friends, they all eagerly, and perhaps just a little too eagerly, volunteered to go get my clothes from outside of the shower truck so I could get dressed.

We made it to our CAT II group photo with time to spare. We chatted a bit with fellow riders and took the picture. When the group disbursed, Jeanne and I were stuck deciding what to do. It took a very short time to decide we both desperately just wanted to lie around, so we ended up taking a nap. It was nice to go to sleep with all the activity around me.

I set the alarm for an hour and a half, but I woke almost a half hour early. I just lay there and watched the people outside of the tent, listened to the conversations nearby, and watched Jeanne scrunch her face up in her sleep. Mostly I just thought about my wife, and my kids, and I wondered what they were doing. It was so odd I was now in a completely different world than all of them. Day Five was over, and I still couldn't believe I was here, and as much as I missed my wife and family, I was saddened the ride was almost over.

After Jeanne woke, we decided to visit the Dedication Tent. I had teased Jeanne about being emotional throughout the ride, and of course she wept in the Dedication Tent, but I didn't give her any grief this time. I was deeply moved to see what others had written about their loved ones, some gone and some still living.

Dinner would be special tonight. Lea Delaria had come to provide entertainment for us, or as she so elegantly put it, she was there to "Bob Fuckin' Hope" us. She sang a few jazz songs, did some hysterical stand up, and then emceed our talent show.

Just as she began the show, Lea made an announcement that the photographer would like to take a photo of all "the people of color." She made some comment about everything having to be so politically correct, and it made me laugh. After determining that I was, in fact, "of color," I went out with that group. It took a while for the photographer to meet us, so while we were all waiting, I joked there actually was no picture to be taken, and that this was just a ruse to have us all leave so the others could tell racist jokes comfortably.

When I went back in, the show had begun. The first performer of the evening was a young girl who had missed her high school graduation to do the ride. Dressed in Cap and Gown, she played the Star Spangled Banner on her flute, and we all sang along. It was one of the most moving moments of the ride for me.

Then, for some reason, Lea apologized to us for her comment about political correctness. Apparently someone had taken great offense, and Lea wanted to make it clear she hadn't wanted to offend anyone.

Timing really is everything, as the next performer was a young white man who chose to sing for us, and his selection would be from the stage version of "Showboat" (or maybe it was the movie version, I don't really remember). And then he began "Ol' Man River, that oooold man river"....and he went on, "he must know sumpin" ...and on "he don't plant taters..." Yup...he just kept rolling along. And when he was done we broke into thunderous applause!

Most of the talent show acts were pretty good. Some were pretty funny. Some folks were actually talented. Some folks read poetry or did other readings. My friend Lloyd Carrera made me cry when he did his reading. In part he said:

> *In the last twenty years, over 538,795 people have died of AIDS in the U.S. alone. My brother Larry Carrera, was one of them. He came to live in my family's home where we cared for him until he died. My mother and I had the immeasurable blessing of holding my brother in our arms as he took his last breath and entered into eternity. He joined my father, who had died just a year and a half before.*
>
> *This is my 3rd AIDS ride. I have never been concerned about the financial challenge of the rides, because I believe in people and knew the response would be generous...and it has been. All 3 rides combined, I have raised over $20,000.00 for AIDS*

Charities. I wasn't too concerned about the physical challenge, because I knew, after my first training ride, that I could do it with all the support, love and encouragement of my fellow riders. I was concerned though, about the emotional challenge I would be facing... the surfacing of faded memories, Larry's struggle for life, then death... and the still fresh pain of losing a brother to this horrific disease...

...But with each turn of the pedals, for these 585 miles of rigorous cycling ...I am remembering my brother, Larry, who is the wind against my back.

With each beat of my heart, I thank God for his life and mine, and remember the hundreds of thousands of people this ride is helping.

Since then, and forever more, any time I feel a tailwind, I think of Lloyd's brother, Larry.

I was really shaken by another speaker, and one particular line. When I asked for help with this ride, donations came from many generous folks, of many denominations, including Christians. But I was shocked by the response of a few folks who call themselves "Christian" and in the name of their Christianity, felt they could, and in fact should, ignore certain segments of the population who are in need. I consider myself a Christian and so I was happy to hear this young man when he posed the question:

What would Jesus do? What would JESUS DO? I'll tell you what Jesus would do! JESUS WOULD DO THE FUCKING RIDE!!! If Jesus were around today he'd be right here with us!

211

As uncomfortable as I was to hear the name of my Lord used in the same sentence as the "F" word, this guy hit the nail on the head for me. He said exactly what I'd wanted to say several times now, but could never put into words. There have been few occasions in my life in which I have felt closer to God, than the days I spent on the ride.

By the time the show was over and we headed back to our tents, it was very dark, and later than any night before. Laurie was concerned that I called so late, and we got shushed faster than usual and I said goodnight.

So in the end, our one free afternoon of the week was spent sleeping. Next year Jeanne and I might have to ride as "Team Excitement!"

The Quints from left…Kate Topolski, Michelle Seith, Kim Baker, Ann Miller and Courtney Pearson

Day Six was the last full day, and I have to say I was sad to see my time on the ride slipping away. My rear end, on the other hand, was quite happy this disaster was nearly over, and would rather have been anywhere else than on a bicycle seat.

Everywhere around me there were signs the ride had taken its toll on many folks. They were taped, wrapped, limping and burnt. Tilmin told us later the glitter from her outfit on Day five hadn't been such a good idea. Apparently she had gotten "glitter in places glitter shouldn't go." And she quickly learned glitter can be quite abrasive. For Day Six, Tilmin was out of the ride and working in a sag truck, because as she so delicately phrased it, her "coochie" was "on fire."

Tilmin also made the front page of the Riders Digest Today, which is only two pages, so I guess she had a fifty/fifty chance of making it on the front page. Apparently she was trying to reattach a fingernail with the glue from her tube patch kit. She was advised it wouldn't work, and she shouldn't try it with false eyelashes either.

We were back to our five AM routine on Day Six. It was, by now, very routine, and I was quite used to it. Today was unofficially "Spongebob Squarepants" day. It started pretty much because our friend and fellow rider, Lydia Winkeller, made the mistake of saying how much she disliked Spongebob, and some of her friends took that as a challenge.

If you're not familiar with Spongebob, you obviously don't have small children. He is a little cartoon character who is pretty much a sponge with appendages and a face. He lives in a pineapple under the sea (!?), and spends time with his starfish buddy, Patrick.

Recently, Focus on the Family founder Dr. James C. Dobson, has been cited in the press as accusing Spongebob of being gay. In all fairness to Dr. Dobson, he never actually said Spongebob was gay. I read Dr. Dobson's February 2005 newsletter, entitled "Setting the Record Straight." One might think Dr. Dobson has a sense of humor, but my guess would be he missed this pun entirely. In my opinion, what Dr. Dobson actually said is far more sinister and scary than simply outing Spongebob.

Laurie had made a special Spongebob Jersey for me out of sponge appliqués from a kid's art project. On the back of my jersey, there was a picture of Patrick carrying Spongebob. The message beneath the picture said "He ain't heavy, he's my Spongebob." I would spend the entire day thanking fellow riders for their compliments on that jersey.

We ran into the quints in bike parking. They had endeared themselves to us time and time again on this journey. I wanted to make sure to get a picture with them.

I think it was on Day Four, I had been hoping our lunch stop would have asphalt to sit on. It's funny how much your standards can be lowered in just a week. I wasn't even hoping for lawn, as that seemed unrealistic. To my great joy and amazement, the lunch stop had picnic tables!

Almost as soon as I made that discovery, Kate the quint came over and told us "All the cool people are over here." To which I replied, "Oh, then I guess we better sit over there!" She was really sincere in her invitation to join her and her young friends, but we were too enthralled by the picnic tables, and therefore, declined.

I told the quints to go home and tell their parents what a fine job they'd done raising such wonderful young women. If they forgot, and if you're the parent of a quint, I'm telling you now, nice work!

Back on the road again, the drawback to the Spongebob appliqués was their rubber backing. My skin wasn't breathing under the rubber, and so my back was sweating profusely. I don't know if it was physiological, or just psychological, but I couldn't get enough to drink between rest stops. Normally, a bottle of Gatorade and a water bottle were more than enough between stops. On Day Six, while the day was cool and overcast, that amount just wasn't cutting it.

I was also concerned with Jeanne's hydration. She was drinking water, but she had stopped drinking Gatorade on Day Five because she felt it was giving her a sore throat and sore tongue. While drinking water is important, electrolyte replacement is essential as well. I had brought plenty of Gu shots, and we had used them sparingly thus far, so I was encouraging her to do the shots. She didn't do as many as I would have liked, but she never slowed down, and she continued to ride well.

Early in the day, Jeanne noticed my rear tire was low, and when I checked, it registered less than 50 lbs. per square inch. I pumped it back up to 110 lbs. and we rode on, but within an hour or so it was low again. We stopped and changed the tube, and that was it, my only flat of the ride. Miraculously, that would be our last mechanical problem, and so the total damage between us for the week was one broken water bottle cage, two broken spokes, two flats, and a broken helmet mirror. We couldn't have asked for better.

We had great tailwinds almost the entire day. We had much more traffic to deal with than we had in the past, and we also had more folks cheering us on. Often, mothers with small children would be sitting on their porches cheering and clapping, or sometimes you might see kids sitting on their back fences waving to us. Almost all the riders waved back, and Jeanne and I would always squeak our dumb little horns to express our thanks. I remember the little town of Carpinteria being especially warm and friendly to us.

At some point during the day, Jeanne asked if we could stop at a store. For a long while now the only stores we had seen were very small general stores in tiny towns. Today we saw an actual supermarket. Jeanne hadn't volunteered what she needed to buy, and I know better than to ask. I watched our bikes and those of a couple of other Riders while Jeanne shopped. The store had nice little café tables outside, and so I positioned myself at a table where I could keep an eye on all the bikes.

While I was waiting, many shoppers asked me about all of the riders and where we were going, and from where had we come, and why were we riding. I was really proud to tell them all about the AIDS/LifeCycle, and they were amazed to hear we had ridden all the way from San Francisco.

Jeanne came out of the store pulling a huge bottle of mouth wash from the store bag and transferring it to her bike pack. It was a lot of extra weight for her to carry, especially considering I had a small bottle of mouth wash in my Hygiene bag, which I would have happily given to her to put in her Hyruss bag had I known she needed it. She said she wanted to try to get rid of the trench mouth which had been plaguing her. In spite of the huge amount of time we had spent together, it seems we really didn't have that much time to communicate.

217

Jeanne had also purchased what she called "the best Coke" she ever had in her life, and a diet Coke for me. We sat and enjoyed the table and chairs for a moment.

Just inside Santa Barbara we began to see signs making reference to our friend Lydia Winkeller, who is from Santa Barbara and has many friends and family there. The signs would say things like "Go Lydia! You're almost there!" or "Lydia and the ALC Riders rock!" It was pretty cute.

Then, we began to see signs for the legendary "Paradise Pit." Signs reading "No Clif Bars!" or "Gatorade free zone" were welcome sights to us, as we had been eating and drinking way too much of both all along the ride. One sign said "Better than Brad Pitt...Paradise Pitt."

Paradise pit is a long-standing tradition manned by local saints who served ice cream (all you can eat), cookies and fresh strawberries! It was as close to heaven as I'd been in six days.

Later, back on the road, I was riding a pretty nice downhill. There was a good amount of traffic, and we were all being careful to watch out for cars. I am very cautious not to follow other riders too closely, occasionally excepting Jeanne, and then only into a headwind at low speeds. I usually keep a couple of bike lengths between myself and the next rider. This proved to be my saving grace.

As we were riding a downhill at about 25 mph, a car turned right into a parking lot, cutting off the rider in front of me. The driver failed to signal, and appeared to notice us only after he was halfway across our path, at which point he slammed on his brakes and stopped dead. The rider in front of me hit his brakes as he had no other alternative but to veer into heavy vehicular traffic. He went into a sideways slide, ending up with both feet down inches from the car. He actually pushed off the vehicle with his hand to keep from falling. He was face to face with the right rear passenger, who had the most terrified look on his face! Had the window been down, my fellow rider could easily have smooched the kid in the back seat, but I'm fairly certain that was the farthest thing from either of their minds. I broke hard as well, and slid sideways, ending parallel to the rider in front of me and about two feet from him, and I'll admit I cursed as I slid, to no one in particular.

Even though there was a good distance between us, big guys can't stop as fast as smaller guys, especially downhill. I guess when I yelled, my fellow rider thought I was upset with him, and as we started up again, he apologized to me. I told him; on the contrary, I was grateful to him for his skill, and his cat-like reflexes. Had I been in his position, there is no question in my mind but that the incident would have ended in my serious injury, and I told him as much.

There was nothing else he, or I for that matter, could have done. We were being cautious, paying close attention and traveling in a bike lane about ten mph under the speed limit, with a safe distance between us, and we had a very near miss. We put it behind us and rode on.

It wasn't long afterwards I was stopped at a light and I heard a female voice behind me yell "ON YOUR...STOPPING ...WATCH OUT!" and I felt an arm slamming across my shoulder blades. A very pretty young woman had failed to unclip and had used me to stop her, and to stop her fall. She apologized profusely, and then, there we were at the light, her with her arm around me, and me feeling a bit uncomfortable. As she was leaning towards me, and too close to me to unclip and put her foot down, we really couldn't untangle until the light turned green and she could ride on. If I wasn't a big fat guy, we'd have both been on the pavement. We introduced ourselves and made very awkward conversation for the duration of what seemed like a very long light.

This was the last day for Rest Stop 4, and their finale was as wonderful as anything they had done all week. They all wore dazzling Swan Lake costumes, white leotards with white tutus, and white feather headpieces. As we rode in, they would stand in a ballet position with one arm over their head, and then bow in unison as we passed. It was a hysterical sight, and just as they had as "the Secret Service," they maintained their straight faces, as if they took their ballet horribly seriously.

For me, the picture of the week was at Rest Stop 4 on Day Six. One of the "ballerinas" was changing a CD in a boom box. He bent over in a most un-ladylike pose, grabbing the boom box, and exposing his tighty whiteys peaking out from under his leotard. It was just fortunate I had my camera handy.

We rode along the coast all day. The sea was beautiful, the tailwinds were excellent, and the weather was overcast and cool.

I couldn't have hoped for better. Still, my rear was hurting like never before, and there was no longer a comfortable secondary riding position. Everything down there hurt, and the only way I could have been comfortable on a bike by this time would have been standing on my hands. It goes without saying, everyone else felt exactly as I did by then.

I remember at some point during the day, there was some confusion over the route. Several people were calling out, asking "Which Way?" I looked around and couldn't make heads or tails out of the markings. A fellow rider called out "Follow the ass in front of you!" It wasn't a very comforting thought, but I looked around, picked out an ass, and started riding, and darned if it didn't work out!

Rest Stop 4, Day Six…Swan Lake Greeting
(Photo Courtesy of Shelly Ross)

We made it in our last full day and we were greeted by more folks than we had on any previous day, except perhaps Day One. There were many extra people as I guess many riders from Southern California had relatives greeting them there.

Our day ended on the beach in Ventura, with a candlelight vigil by the ocean. We all stood quietly, silently, except for me fumbling with my camera trying to capture the moment in a video, and the thud of Jeanne ramming her elbow into my ribs to make me stop. It really was a beautiful moment, and I'll remember it forever. There were probably 2,000 people holding candles in a circle, and all you could hear was the crashing of the waves.

I'm sure most people were thinking about loved ones they had lost to the AIDS pandemic, and I was thinking about all the new friends I have met who are HIV-positive. I prayed I'll be riding with them until the victory ride, and not remembering them at a vigil.

After a time, we all walked back to our tents, putting ourselves in our sleeping bags for the last time. Between the vigil, and the last goodnight, the mood was quite somber.

Kate's Story

Sometimes people shared their reasons for riding with us while we participated in training rides, and some people shared their stories on the ride itself. Just before I completed this book, and after I'd done training rides with her for nearly a year, Kathryn (Kate the Quint) Topolski sent me an e-mail in which she shared her story.

Kate and her Mom

In Memory of Sheila Casey Topolski

by Kate Topolski

222

My mother was born December 17, 1946, and grew up to be an excellent athlete. She loved tennis and badminton with her team of sisters, as well as skiing and waterskiing. My mother was also a smart woman. She studied hard, earning the grades at Fresno State College to become a lab scientist at a hospital in San Francisco, where she worked for years and saved her money to take trips abroad to experience European food, art, and culture.

She met my father in San Francisco, got married, and made a home in Mill Valley. I was born in 1979, and my sister came along two years later. My mother loved chemistry and cooking, which she saw as the same thing. And she had a sense of adventure. She took me to museums and musicals and would always know a great nook where you could find a steaming pork bow or some other food from a distant corner of the world. She always made me feel special and loved-as if we had our own secret between us.

In the mid eighties she received a letter from the hospital stating that she needed to be tested for AIDS because a transfusion she received shortly after my sister was born may have been tainted (it was). Our parents waited years before sharing the news with my sister and me because they wanted to protect us from the stigma associated with the disease early on in its history. My mother's background in chemistry allowed her to work closely with the doctors throughout her treatment, providing important feedback on the effects of treatment, but in 1994, my mother's body couldn't hold out any longer. The years of medication took a toll and her liver began to fail. On that hot summer day she left us, I felt relieved, at least her physical suffering was over and now she could take care of us in peace.

Losing such a strong figure in my life has been difficult, and I have often felt lost. Growing up I never felt I could share this story, that it was too heavy to burden someone with or that no one would understand. I was scared I'd get emotional and so I buried my voice.

Then I found AIDS/LifeCycle. Suddenly I was part of a community who shared my experiences of grief and loss, yet cycled to give and celebrate life. They were riding for their own lives, for the lives of their loved ones, and of loved ones lost. Together we raised 5 million dollars in 2004 and 6.8 million in 2005, and that will give "a person another walk along the beach, another sunset, another date, another laugh, another dance, another hug, another chance."

I would like to recognize my mother, who taught me everything I know about strength and courage and who summoned enough of these traits to raise my sister and me with love and values that will guide us for all of our lives.

February 24, 2004

Dear Mom,

I've registered for AIDS/LifeCycle, a 585 mile ride from San Francisco to L.A. that takes place this coming June. I have thought about participating before but I wasn't ready for it until now. As you know this is much more than a physical challenge or fundraising goal for me. When you contracted HIV from a tainted blood transfusion in the early eighties, our lives changed forever. Why did you and tens of thousands of others have to contract HIV through blood transfusions before donated blood was properly screened? The thought of it makes me angry, then I feel helpless and sad because there is nothing I or anyone can do to change the past.

Your life was taken too early ten years ago and I think of all the things I haven't been able to share with you and won't get to share with you in person. I think about how different our family is without you. But what I realize now is that I can't get stuck in the silence, pain, and grief of the past, I must move forward and do something. Like the virus itself, I must be flexible and changing, and channel my angry and sad emotions into helping others so that HIV and AIDS will not affect more and more families the way it affected ours. Now that I am ready, AIDS/LifeCycle has given me the forum to do this. I am raising money to educate, to help people with HIV and AIDS, to support families, and to make expensive life extending drugs, like the ones that thankfully helped you survive for so many years, accessible. I expect the physical aspect of the ride to be cathartic for me and it couldn't be in a more supportive environment. I know you will be with me every pedal of the way.

Love you and miss you,

Kate

Photo Courtesy of Shelly Ross

As of this writing there are **47,908,618 people living with HIV/AIDS.**
Since 1981, **37,202,550 people have died** from HIV/AIDS.
Young people (15-24 years old) account for **half of all new HIV infections.**

By December 2003, **women accounted for nearly 50%** of all people living with HIV worldwide.
In 2003, an estimated **500,000 children** under the age of 15 died from **HIV/AIDS.**

Worldwide, **fourteen million children have been orphaned by AIDS.**
That's the equivalent of every child under the age of five in the United States.

In the very brief time it took you to read this page, 8 people have been infected with HIV and 5 people have died from HIV/AIDS.

Bike Parking, bikes with eggs, Day Seven
(Courtesy Shelly Ross and The Chicken Lady)

Day Seven - Ventura to Los Angeles

Day Seven started a bit differently than most, in that I reclaimed the stuff I had kept in Jeanne's bag during the week. Her bag was much larger than mine and she had spare space, while my smaller bag was stuffed to the gills, and we were afraid the zippers would burst. We rolled our mats for the last time, packed our stuff, and turned in our tent, which had been our home for the past week.

While we were gathering our things, I watched two women clinging to each other, and saying a very sad farewell. They were crying uncontrollably, kissing and holding each other, and my heart broke for them both. My heart was a bit broken anyway.

We had camped very near the beach, and our stuff was cold and wet. Our last breakfast together was bittersweet. We had all been family for seven days, and we all hated to say goodbye. Still, our heads were reeling with the thoughts of a real bed and real porcelain, but mostly of our loved ones at home.

We headed out to bike parking. Today was another short day, only 60 miles, but the route closed at 3:00 instead of 7:00, and so I still took the day's route seriously. Besides, today was the first day I actually began to believe I was going to complete every inch of the ride.

If you're into bicycles, bike parking is truly beautiful. It's a sea of every imaginable shape, style, and color of bike, row after row, which goes on almost as far as the eye can see. Today though, we were treated to a very special sight.

There were 1,616 riders who started this venture. Rumor has it 1602 completed the ride in one fashion or another. On Day Seven, every single bicycle seat had a plastic egg banded to it, courtesy of the Chicken Lady. Each egg had the words "ALC Hero" written on it. Inside mine was a mint, and a tiny rolled scroll which looked like a miniature diploma.

After the preparation which all of us had undertaken, and after the fundraising struggles we all shared, I can't imagine the dedication it takes to go beyond all that and prepare the thousands of eggs the Chicken Lady delivered. I can't adequately describe the difficulty of carrying a plate of food after you've ridden more than five hundred miles in six days, and this man, this true hero, managed to have more than 1,600 plastic eggs banded to bike seats sometime between the evening of Day Six and the morning of Day Seven. Tears welled in my eyes when I thought of the sacrifice this guy made to inspire and motivate us. Not wanting to fall apart and have a big sobbing breakdown publicly, I didn't open my scroll until later. When I did it said:

he-ro n., pl. heroes One who commits to taking 7 days out of their lives to ride a bicycle to help raise money for services to help those living with HIV/AIDS. One with no fear. One who wants to make a difference. One who is giving a person another walk along the beach, another sunset, another date, another laugh, another dance, another hug, another chance. One as a figure, a legend renowned for exceptional courage and fortitude.

YOU, are a hero! Thank you, Chicken Lady ALC4 Rider #3011

Thank you Ken Thomason! You are a true hero!

I have a special egg holder for my plastic green/blue egg. It sits in a special place in my home, displayed for all to see. I unrolled my scroll to copy the above text, and rolled it back up, put it back in its little pink ribbon, and then placed it back in my green/blue plastic egg, alongside the mint. In my life I've received my share of awards, but I only display one.

As we began our day's ride this last time, we were pretty keyed up. There was no doubt we had the muscle and endurance to finish, it was now only a question of avoiding mishap or mechanical failure. We rode carefully and slowly at first, warming up as usual.

Before we returned to Highway 1, Jeanne and I couldn't resist the temptation to veer off the course and try out a restroom at a public park in Ventura. It wasn't porcelain, but it was the first flushing noise we'd heard in a week. I joked I was just going to hang out and flush for a while. Before we left we were joined by other like-minded riders.

Between the tailwinds and the adrenaline, the pace picked up quickly, and before we knew it we were back on Highway 1 and at Rest Stop 1. The mood was jovial. It was another quick in and out. There were only twelve miles now to Rest Stop 2. I had been worried we would be cutting it close with a 3:00 route closing, but it was becoming evident that barring a major tragedy, we were all but there.

Still, we've seen our share of tragedies. We'd seen other riders crash hard, we'd had our own minor spills, and a few near misses. There was nothing to say we wouldn't have nine flats today, as we had one weekend. We took nothing for granted, and I wouldn't feel secure until I was close enough to the end of The Ride to carry my bike over the finish line in the allotted time.

Taking a hill somewhere on the road on Day 7

Rest Stop 2 was manned by angels. It was so apropos, as I had felt every rest stop, and every water stop, and all the stops along the way were manned by angels. They were dressed as pirates, toys, tramps, cowboys, pit crews, French maids, harem girls, rock stars, the Von Trapps, the Secret Service, Dolly Partons, witches, mermaids, characters from Oz, swans, ladybugs, and angels, but let me tell you...Every single one of these people were angels and treated me with kindness and caring and love. I may have forgotten to mention some of their themes, but I will never forget their benevolence and their love. It wasn't just rest stop and lunch folks who were wonderful either. Every single Roadie, from the bike parking guy to the big guy with the pearl earrings who served me dinner every night, Ginger and Scott cheering us up the hills, the gear truck people (please forgive us!), the folks who laid out the tent

231

grid, to the people who cleaned up camp after we moved on, every single Roadie was incredibly compassionate!

I remember back when my daughters were babies. I remember feeding them in the middle of the night and rocking them, and honestly, babies are pretty useless creatures. They can't change your oil for you, or do the dishes, or anything else. They pretty much just cry and eat and go to the bathroom, and cause you a lot of work, and yet you love them so much! This is the purest love I have ever given in my life, because I absolutely knew there was nothing in it for me.

As best as I can describe it, as a Rider, that's how I felt loved by the Roadies. We Riders had nothing to give the Roadies but maybe a smile and a thank you, and yet, those roadies just loved us up, and cared for us, and worked for us, and provided for us. Their sacrifice was no less than ours, but until Day Seven, nobody cheered them on.

As we rode out from Rest Stop 2, a beautiful young woman, who very much reminded me of my daughter Megan, stood by the side of the road and held a sign which said "Highway to Heaven." That sign touched me on a couple of different levels.

The Pacific Coast Highway was beautiful and the ocean was stunning, rolling in every shade of blue and green imaginable. In some places we rode so close we could feel the ocean spray as we passed. The weather was foggy and overcast, just the way I like it when I'm riding hard. Unfortunately, the traffic was heavy, and scary. I saw a couple of near misses, and a few swerving drivers. I was very uneasy.

At one point I saw a car making a dangerous "U" turn, and from my vantage point, it almost looked like he was intentionally aiming at Julie Brown. Julie displayed incredible bike skills, and it was only her experience and proficiency which kept her from disaster as she nimbly dodged the errant motorist.

We managed to ride it out to lunch, which was at Malibu Lagoon State Beach. We pulled in, looked around, and wanting to avoid another ALC sandwich, I suggested we look for a restaurant or something nearby. We turned around, crossed the road, and found a small deli. Leaving our bikes with some fellow riders outside, we waited in the deli line for a while before we realized we had to get a number. I gave my order to Jeanne, and went back out to try to get a table.

Though Jeanne was in line for a long time, not one table had cleared. I was really hoping that we could sit at an actual table, but I had resigned myself to the idea we'd have to get comfortable on asphalt. But when Jeanne returned, some of our fellow riders, who were nearly done with their meal, gave us their table. I'm sure they still wanted to do some resting and chatting, but they generously cut their rest short for us. We were very grateful for their consideration.

I don't know where they went, but they asked us to keep an eye on their stuff and their bikes. We'd known them for all of 90 seconds and they left us watching their bikes, and left their wallets on the table. At this point in The Ride, I didn't find that the least bit unusual.

Jeanne and I enjoyed two of the best meat loaf sandwiches ever created. We enjoyed the leisurely pace at which we ate. We enjoyed watching other people who weren't wearing spandex or helmets.

I imagine we couldn't have looked or smelled all that pretty by then, and some of the civilians looked uncomfortable with our presence. Others, though, asked about our ride, and our cause, and I was always very proud to talk about it.

The other riders returned and picked up their bikes and stuff, and headed out. Once we completed our meal, we began the chapter of our ride which might be called "In search of Porcelain." We were not to be denied, and at a mall across a small street, we found the nicest public bathroom in California. It was lovely!

Word soon spread amongst our fellow riders like wild fire, and before Jeanne made it through the ladies line, there was a pretty sizable queue behind her. The men's line was forming quickly as well. The bathrooms could accommodate only one person at a time, and each time the door opened, all the riders would crane their necks or stretch to the side of the line to catch a glimpse of the white.

As bathroom lines will tend to do, they soon became uneven, with the ladies line doubling the men's. Some ladies debated whether to wait in the longer line to use an actual "ladies room." Others quickly jumped ship and switched lines. The civilians were appalled. They couldn't possibly know some of these same women had been squatting in thorny weeds to avoid port-a-potties for an entire week now.

For the very last time (this year...yes we will almost surely be back next year) we hit the road down the homestretch, more cautious than ever. We had 15 miles left, and as one Rider put it, we could smell the barn. Adrenaline was at an all time high for me, and it was everything I could do not to try to sprint to the finish.

About seven miles from the completion of the ride, we were once again reminded that finishing was not assured. We watched a fellow rider being loaded into an ambulance, his friends looking on. I can only imagine what a huge disappointment that would be, and the mood around us became somber.

At mile 56, with four miles remaining, we came to an underpass which required us to dismount, carry our bicycles down stairs, walk our bikes through a very long and dark tunnel, and then carry them back upstairs. We, of course, handled this obstacle in the same dignified and mature manner we had shown throughout the week. Once we were inside the dark tunnel, a chorus of spooky noises sprang forth. Some folks wailed like ghosts, women screamed, maniacal laughter came from the far end of the tunnel.

As we emerged on the opposite side, we became hysterical as we watched two young teenaged girls about to enter the tunnel from that side, and the faces they made upon hearing the debacle below were priceless. We assured them the group was harmless.

Very shortly thereafter we climbed a small hill, and Shelly was there waiting. She took my picture as she told me this was "THE LAST HILL" and for some reason, this time I believed her. This was the first time I knew I was going to finish, because at this point, if my bike broke in half, I still had time to carry that bastard over the finish line if need be.

With less than three miles left to go, many riders had stopped at local establishments. I surmised they were choosing to wait the rest of the time enjoying Jamba Juice, as opposed to more Gatorade at the finish line. Maybe next year I'll feel that way too, but at that point, I wanted nothing more than to finish The Ride.

The greeters started long before the VA hospital at the end, but the closer we got, the more there were. By the time we got to the finish, the crowd was huge, and I felt like I had just won the Tour de France. We pulled in about 1:00 PM, more than two hours early. Tears were streaming down my face as I rode in, and Jeanne was crying uncontrollably. We spotted her sister, Jerie, in the crowd right away, and she came over to join us. Jeanne and I congratulated each other and hugged with the same "Oh my God, we did it! I can't believe it!" enthusiasm which we shared on our first century, times ten! I don't know how we didn't hurt each other or Jerie hugging, and I have no idea how many times we pointed at each other and said "EFI baby!" or "I can't believe we did it!"

But we did it…We rode every inch of The Ride, and we rode every hill without stopping.

The feeling of accomplishment was completely and totally overwhelming and all-consuming. Months later, it's hardly faded, if at all. All through the day, and the evening, and the ride home the next day, Jeanne and I kept looking at one another and saying, "I can't believe we did it!" I still haven't grasped the reality that I actually made it!

The tears flowed for a while, and I left the sisters McArthur so they could have a moment. I called my wife Laurie first. She didn't answer, so I left a message, and kept calling everyone in my family until somebody answered, and after I babbled and blubbered with them for a while, I'd call somebody else.

There is no describing the feeling of achievement and pure elation when you complete The Ride. If I think of that finish a million times, and remember watching my brother and sister riders finishing that ride, I'll never fail to get choked up. It was truly the realization of a dream!

As I watched the Riders finish, and as I watched each express their exuberance, I wondered what brought them to this point. Some surely were bikers, racers, maybe just here for a challenge and at the same time, to serve a good cause. Others might have been athletes in high school or college and are here on a new challenge.

Those I've talked with lead me to believe the majority of participants on The Ride weren't athletes at all…ever. I'd guess there were many former band geeks, drama freaks, and chess club members represented on The Ride. Some I know were the kids who were picked last in P.E. or maybe didn't even "suit up."

Many were folks who some would say have no business doing a ride like this. They started this journey with nothing more going for them than a desire to do something good, perhaps to honor a loved one who had passed, or in hopes of keeping a loved one alive.

And then there were those riders who were clearly too sick to be making this journey, but they made it anyway. They walked their bikes up most hills, inspiring us, and bringing tears to our eyes.

Jeanne and I rejoined, got drinks (vitamin water, not Gatorade!), got some snacks, and picked up our "Victory" shirts. I was under the impression all the same colors rode into closing ceremonies together, so we had to agree on a color. Jeanne wanted purple, and I didn't care that much, so purple it was. As it turns out we didn't have to get the same color, but in retrospect, I'm glad we did. We are road partners, Jeanne and I. We started this thing together, and we finished it together, and if my buddy Jeanne wants to wear the most effeminate colored purple shirt that mankind ever created, well damn it, I'm right there with her! Jeanne couldn't possibly have been a better tentmate, or a better friend. No matter who we ride with in the future, she will always be my first road partner for my first ALC, and I'll never forget that.

After we grabbed our shirts, we went back to cheer in our fellow riders. We finished long before many other riders, not because we're faster, but because we didn't stop for tea or Jamba Juice. And what of our fellow riders you may ask?

They all lived happily ever after. Most of them rode in worn, but healthy and safe. We saw Jane and Karen "C" ass along the ride, but I never saw them at the finish. They were looking good and strong on the road, so my guess is they did well. We saw Psycho Alan on Day One, but he was struggling with a bad cold, and was regretting riding that day. We never saw him again, and we assumed he couldn't finish, due to his illness. But On March 26, 2006 Jeanne and I bumped into Alan, and he told us he too had ridden every inch. We were ecstatic all over again.

George Harrison and Jeanne, who is apparently throwing down gang signs while doing her impression of Shirley Temple

Jeanne's good friend Edna, who was a TRL on the Punch and Pie Ride and led us in Brady Bunch trivia pursuit, was unable to do the ride for personal reasons. She was there to help out on Day Zero though, and was with us in spirit every day. Jeanne carried all Edna's tent chips from previous rides with her throughout The Ride along with a recording of Edna's giggle.

Jeanne's friend Dellma, who rode with us on Day on The Ride for our first Century, was also unable to make ALC 4. Just a week or so before The Ride, Dellma was involved in a serious cycling accident while training on Mount Diablo. Her injuries were rather severe, but our thoughts were with her on the ride as well. I hope she'll make it next year.

We saw George Harrison and our friend Kurt soon after we finished. We saw Joseph, Julie Brown, Alan and Stephanie finish. We saw both Hudson sisters, Kelly and Tilmin, come in, and I got a picture of them together. Sue Lackey, and her Road Partner, David, rode in safely and we exchanged hugs all around. By the way, Randy Barber, who was a Training Ride Leader on the Three Bears training ride, rode moto-crew and I saw him every day, and every day he encouraged me. Ben and all the quints made it in safely. We thanked Ben for all his work training us, and he gave us a big hug. I heard rumor the quints already signed up for next year.

The Sisters Hudson at the finish, Kelly and Tilmin

Shelly had a good ride until Day Seven. I saw her from a distance and cheered wildly for her. Like many people, Shelly was crying. But I could tell something was wrong, and I could see no victory smile. Shelly told us that after a blowout, just a mile from the finish line, her front tire locked up and she went over her bars. She scrubbed badly, making her miserable as she finished, but she's already signed up for next year, and I have no doubt she'll be there.

As luck would have it, when we got in line for closing ceremonies, we were lined up with the quints, and we chatted while we waited. We had enjoyed their company and kindness all along the ride so it was fitting we should end it with them.

The closing ceremonies were both inspiring and funny. First, the Riders came in and were divided into two groups. We got in our places, which left a huge aisle in the center. Then the Roadies walked in through that opening, and there was mass pandemonium. This was our opportunity to let our Roadies know how much we appreciated them.

As they passed through we clapped and cheered and whistled and honked our stupid little horns. Some Riders sprayed the Roadies with their water bottles. I kept thinking about the backwash, and besides I was out of water. This was the biggest, loudest, most raucous ovation of the ride, and I think the Roadies got the message. The closing ceremony also included the members of the Positive Pedalers escorting the riderless bike, which represents all those lost to the AIDS pandemic. There was hardly a dry eye in the house.

Before the ceremony ended, we were all asked to remember The Ride, and to take the spirit of The Ride with us. I try to do that in my day to day life, but I just can't bring myself to leave all my money in a pack, unattended in the middle of 2,000 people. Somehow, it's just not the same, and I have to tell you, when you've lived The Ride for a week, returning to reality takes some getting used to.

Then, just like that…it was over.…

We searched around and found our gear, and then made the long trek back to Jeanne's truck, which Jerie had driven from San Mateo. As we all headed back to our vehicles, Jeanne commented it was like the movie "Godspell," where all the people were "called," but then at the end of the movie they all resume their normal lives.

I have to say I was honored to ride with this group. For seven days we were a Utopian little society in which everyone cared for, and watched out for, one another. I never asked for help with anything and didn't receive it, and I often got help before I asked or even thought of asking. This has been true from the moment I signed up for this ride.

I came away from this event feeling a greater resolve and sense of commitment, and I expect I'll be riding in AIDS/ LifeCycle again next year! I know my money, effort, and time will be put to excellent use, and went to a cause worth the 585 miles I spent on The Ride.

Me

Oh! But the fun doesn't stop there!

The story probably should end here, but I tend to go on and on, and I also tend to exaggerate, and from the fateful ride of '04, until now there's been very little of that, so...

After we hiked what seemed like ten miles back to Jeanne's pick-up, we stood our bikes in Jeanne's snazzy bike rack and we threw our gear into the back of her truck. Jeanne drove, and Jerie offered me shotgun, which I gratefully accepted. You don't realize how much you miss the creature comforts. Jeanne's passenger seat was the first padded chair I had sat on in a week. It was wonderful. Good thing too, as it turned out.

I think it was about ten miles to our motel from the Veteran's Hospital where our ride ended. I was assuming it would be a twenty minute drive. We hopped on one freeway and then transferred to another, and with Tonto McArthur at the wheel, I kicked back, assured we'd arrive at our destination in no time.

Jerie was very confident in her directions, up until a point. In all fairness to Jerie, and I'm only going to be fair this one time, we couldn't go back the way she'd driven to pick us up because one of the major streets she took was a one way street. So we scooted over one block and tried to go up that street, but it veered off to the far end of Los Angeles County somewhere. Jerie suggested we ask those "nice young men over there" for directions. I was busy locking the car doors. All the "nice young men" had spiffy red bandanas. Having already packed my red bandana away, I'd have felt awkward and out of place bothering these "nice young men."

Had I double checked the door locks?

I assured the ladies our hotel was probably just around the corner. Then we drove until we pulled up to a local taqueria. I rechecked the door locks. The ladies asked me to get out and get directions from another bunch of guys who looked a lot like family to me, but my sister, Demi, was a pediatric intensive care nurse in San Jose for a long portion of her career. She has always advised me of three rules, the first being NEVER go to a taqueria. According to Demi, nearly every mother, of nearly every kid who ever got shot, says "Ay! He was just on his way to the taqueria!" The other two rules are never having two beers (I only had a couple of beers) and never mind your own business (I was just minding my own business when...).

Again, I felt we must be really close, and therefore we should just keep driving. Besides, all *these* guys had blue bandanas, and my blue bandana was packed away in my bag. We drove on, but we still didn't get any closer to anything which looked familiar to Jerie, and we were now passing landmarks which shouldn't be familiar for the fourth and fifth time.

Jeanne and Jerie are so sweet and innocent, and once more they suggested I ask those fellows over there for directions, but I know better than to interrupt what appears to be a firearm sale. This is a fairly new rule for me, but I think it's a good one. I checked to make sure the doors were locked, just to make sure.

After about three hours of cruising every bit of turf in Los Angeles County, we decided it might be a good idea to call my wife, have her go online, and mapquest our location and destination, kind of like Mexican Onstar. By now I had worn my power lock button to a nub.

Having visited Los Angeles many times, I know there are hundreds of beautiful neighborhoods there. In our quest to find our motel, Jeanne had somehow managed to avoid most of them.

Laurie handled the search and directions perfectly, and before we knew it we were headed toward a lovely motel...which we passed on the way to our lodgings. Upon finding our accommodations, we parked, and piled out. The place looked okay from the outside, save for the gang graffiti all around the perimeter.

Jeanne had searched the Internet and found a pretty good deal. If you ever need to find a motel like ours, you can go to crackhotels.com. We went inside, and I have to admit the lobby was nice...but then we went to our rooms.

This was my first stay in a motel where the management felt the need to put a metal cage around the housekeeping closet, which was right outside our rooms. It really added to the ambiance of the place. We found out later that the cage was probably in place to keep folks from stealing the lovely half ply toilet tissue, which they supplied in each room at no additional charge. When I opened the door to my room, smoke billowed out like Jeff Spicoli's van in <u>Fast Times at Ridgemont High</u>. Even Jeanne and Jerie were overwhelmed by the smell of smoke in my non-smoking room, and they were already in their room with the door closed behind them.

I knew eventually I'd get used to the smell. We were all far too exhausted to be hassling with getting a new motel, or even a new room. Besides, I had my own bathroom, with my own shower, and my own big mirror with a bunch of huge cracks in it.

We agreed we would shower and change and then go out to find some dinner. I can't tell you how wonderful it was to have my own room or just to take my time getting ready. It was great to be naked without an audience.

I turned on the television, just to hear it, and while it took a while to find an English-speaking channel, once I did, I left the TV on while I showered and changed. Occasionally I'd flush the toilet, just for fun.

The television station was airing a documentary about the survival of a family who was lost at sea for some God-awful amount of time without food or water. Apparently somehow they'd all survived, as they were there talking about their ordeal and describing it for the television cameras. They described the horror they lived through, and all the while I was thinking "Wah! Wah! You bunch of cry babies. Try riding a bike for seven days!" I might have been just a bit punchy.

Somehow we all managed to get ready. I locked my bike to the bed, and went next door to Jeanne and Jerie's. Without going into too much detail, gross things happen when you stay in an 8'X8' tent for a week with someone and travel 585 miles on a bicycle with them. As I've been willing to discuss port-a-potties and butt butter, you can only imagine the things I'm not willing to write about. Anyway, throughout the week, whenever something especially distasteful would come up, the joke was that the offended person would say "are you trying to seduce me?" as Dustin Hoffman said to Anne Bancroft in "The Graduate." This time, Jeanne wanted to show me the filthy wash cloth she'd used. It was brown, but I could tell it used to be white. For the last time I asked "Are you trying to seduce me?" Sadly, Jerie informed us Ms. Bancroft had passed away while we were on the ride. Here's to you, Mrs. Robinson.

The view from my room…really!

We piled back in the pickup and began to look for a place to eat. It took a while, and I was having a bit more sympathy for that family lost at sea. We limited our choices to places in view of the main road, because we knew if we got too far off the path, we'd never find our way back again. We finally decided on, what else, PIZZA! It was heavenly! The beer was perfect! It was, in fact, the perfect meal! I'm not much of a drinker, and the McArthur sisters thought it was pretty funny that after one beer I was feeling no pain, and after two, I was just blind drunk.

Maybe the thing I love most about Jeanne is her sense of humor. She has an incredibly quick wit, and I was finding out her sister Jerie was pretty darn comical herself. The two of them played off one another, as you'd guess they'd been doing it all their lives, and I was thoroughly entertained. And every once in while, in the middle of all that laughter I'd think, "I can't believe we did it!" And sometimes I could tell Jeanne was thinking that too. It was a great celebration!

When we returned to our motel, which we learned was very close to Dodger stadium, it was apparent a game had just let out. Jeanne had to make a left turn through impossible traffic. She finally just forced her way, and we were "home" for the night.

I talked on the phone with Laurie until my cell phone battery died, and then I called her again with my reserve battery. Just being able to talk to Laurie in a normal speaking voice, and for as long as I wanted, was a luxury I hadn't known for a week. We did a lot of catching up.

The drive from L.A. home was pretty uneventful. We had a great time chatting, and I had a great time napping. The McArthur sisters certainly didn't need me to keep them entertained. It was great watching them bounce stories off one another.

The one thing which stands out in my mind is watching the trees swaying in the breeze. The wind had been such an integral part of our lives, dictating our speed and effort. It was so great to see it blowing outside, and for the first time in a week, I didn't care how hard it blew, or what direction.

My homecoming couldn't have been better. Laurie had prepared a big barbecue, and my whole family was there. My wife welcomed me so warmly, I was considering doing another ride the following week. It was almost worth it. We ate, drank, and talked about our big adventure. It was so great to be home!

One would think after spending a solid week keeping constant company with someone, except for those few minutes in showers and port-a-potties, one would be more than ready to say goodbye when it was time to part ways. I felt as if my Siamese twin was being separated from me. Jeanne and I hugged and said goodbye, and that was the last I ever heard from her...until the next day, when we began discussing plans for the Pride Parade.

I'd never been to the Gay Pride Parade. Actually, I believe the official name is the San Francisco Lesbian, Gay, Bisexual, Transgender Pride Parade, but I'd never been to that either.

I've watched it on TV before, and my old truck was actually in the parade once when I loaned it to a friend, who decorated it and made a lovely float out of it. I've always wanted to go, but it's never been a high priority.

The last training ride listed for the year on the training ride calendar, was the shortest of the year. It was the Pride Parade route. ALC would have a contingent of riders in the parade, and all participants, Riders and Roadies were invited to participate.

Even though I'm not gay, I felt this was an opportunity to show support for my LGBT brother and sister riders. Jeanne felt like it was crashing their party. After some discussion, we agreed we would participate.

I wasn't going to write about the "Gay factor," and the ride at all, because it's important to me every person with whom I discuss AIDS understands that **AIDS ISN'T A GAY ISSUE!** In fact, in the year 2004, nearly half of those infected with the HIV virus were straight females.

On the other hand I would be less than honest if I didn't say the Gay and Lesbian populations weren't disproportionately well represented on AIDS/LifeCycle 4. I would also be less than honest if I didn't say I had some slightly uncomfortable moments early on, when I would occasionally be the minority, or even the token straight guy in a sometimes predominantly gay group.

These uncomfortable moments weren't caused by the behavior of anyone else. Without exception everybody involved with The Ride has treated me with the utmost respect, warmth, and caring. No, my awkward feelings were based on my own ignorance and lack of exposure.

I used to think I was a pretty open-minded individual. I'm progressive-thinking, so far as Gay rights are concerned. I can't, for the life of me, understand how same sex marriage denigrates my marriage in any way. When I think of the "gay agenda" which I hear conservatives discuss, I can't help but laugh. For me, "gay agenda" has always conjured up a vision of an itinerary wearing a Carmen Miranda hat and waving a rainbow flag. But maybe that's just me.

Over the course of my training, however, I learned a few things about myself that made me squirm a little. I had some pretty interesting ideas ingrained in me, which I always thought were universal truths, and I didn't like having to second-guess those truths.

I met my friend Alan on the fateful ride of '04, in November, when I rode so poorly and had my failure to unclip crash. Alan was so patient and concerned. My bike Godmother, Shelly, was a Training Ride Leader for that ride, as was Alan. Afterwards, Shelly, Alan and I went out for a burger. We packed all our bikes in the back of my pickup, I got in on the drivers side, and to my shock and horror, Alan jumped in between Shelly and I.

I was fairly certain that where I come from, it's a law or something; if two guys are riding in a pickup with one woman, the woman rides in the center seat. Everyone knows that! Apparently everyone knows that except Alan and Shelly.

A week or two later, Shelly invited me to breakfast with Alan, and I happily accepted, with one stipulation, that Shelly sit in the middle. Shelly thought it was a ridiculous request, but agreed under protest.

I picked up Shelly at her place, and then we drove to pick up Alan. Shelly scooted to the center, and Alan rode "shotgun." Then Shelly asked if we could stop so she could visit one of her animals (remember...Shelly is a pet sitter) and Alan and I waited outside the building. Naturally, while Shelly was inside, Alan scooted to the center of the seat. He didn't even wait for Shelly to come back, so there we were, all snuggled up in my pickup waiting for Shelly. Again, where I come from, this is totally unheard of and I was aghast! We drove to breakfast with Alan sitting in the middle. I figured out I was probably the only person in San Francisco who noticed. By the way, Alan, you can ride in my center seat anytime you like!

I was pretty shaken by same sex kissing as well. Not so much two women. I understand lesbianism. In fact, I can't understand why all women aren't lesbians, but I'm grateful they're not.

Coincidentally, on the day I signed up for the ride, I was fortunate enough to witness a pretty touching exchange between two men, one of whom appeared extremely ill. The healthy man greeted his partner, zipped his coat up higher, raised his collar for him, pulled his hat down lower, and basically bundled up his ailing companion, obviously trying to make him as warm and comfortable as possible. That taken care of, the two men exchanged a kiss which, to my eyes, said far more about love than sexuality. For me, somehow, it was a lesson learned.

When the ALC holiday party came around, I attended with Shelly. Basically, I followed her around like a puppy dog, as I knew almost no one but Shelly, and Shelly knew everyone. I was a bit taken aback to see men greeting each other with a kiss on the cheek. In my culture, maybe you kiss your father on the cheek, or your grandpa, or maybe a revered uncle, but that's about it. My brother Rick kissed me on the cheek when I had my heart attack and he thought I was going to die, but only because he figured if I died, I wouldn't tell anybody. SURPRISE RICK! I only exchange cheek kisses with my closest female friends and family. But there they all were, just casually smooching and greeting and smooching some more.

By May 1st, when I completed my first century, Alan was the first person to greet me. He planted a huge smooch on my cheek, and I barely noticed. Of course I was pretty keyed up and at that point, if Alan blew a raspberry on my tummy, I'd have barely noticed. But since then, a few of my gay friends give me the cheek kiss, and far from taking any kind of offense, I see it as a sign of acceptance.

Some of my new gay friends and acquaintances seem to go out of their way to avoid offending me. On Day Zero I had purchased some gifts for some special ride leaders and friends. One man went to hug me and paused ever so briefly, as if to check if it were okay. I quickly told him "I'm Hispanic, you're gay...I think we're supposed to hug."

I have to say, most times, everyone had a sense of humor about gay/straight relations. One guy looking for a tentmate advertised "I'm gay, but I'm straight tolerant (as long as you act gay in public)."

So, all along this journey, my own old notions had been challenged, and sometimes turned on their head. Now I was getting ready for the Pride Parade.

I was doing the parade for a couple of reasons. First, I take a lot of pride in my AIDS/LifeCycle ride. I am proud of our cause, and I am proud of my accomplishment. Not everyone can say they've ridden a bike from San Francisco to L.A. I'm proud of how hard I trained. I'm proud of my fundraising, and the fact that so many of my friends and family supported me.

Maybe the most important thing I have to offer ALC, though, is that I'm the perfect poster boy to be in a position to say "If I can do it, you can do it!" I think most folks who take one look at me believe this. If I can get just one person to sign on, I'll have made a difference.

The one hesitancy I had about the parade was, in past years when I've watched it, I've been put off by the extreme flamboyancy some participants have displayed. I've always felt that if those darn flamboyant folks could just tone it down a bit, maybe some less tolerant people would be more accepting.

Getting ready for the parade, once again, Laurie stepped up to the plate and helped us out. She decorated our bike wheels with ribbons from every color of, what else, the rainbow. She took the various colored ribbons and ran them around the wheel by running them around each spoke individually. It took her about an hour for each wheel. Then she decorated our helmets with ALC orange and blue curly ribbons, with sparkles, no less. Jeanne and I wore our purple victory shirts, and I have to tell you, we were a sight to behold!

So Laurie and I, Jeanne and Megan, took BART to the city. We piled out on Market Street and found our contingent right away. For the first time, the ALCers disappointed me. I wanted to shout, "Come on people! You're supposed to be Gay!" Jeanne and I were by far the most flamboyant participants from our group.

No matter though. Everyone thought we looked great, and a lot of folks told us they wished they had ribbons like ours on their wheels. I think we looked like a combination of Thing One and Thing Two from The Cat in the Hat, and the Purple People Eater. Most important, though, we had a lot of fun!

Jeanne, myself, and Kate the Quint (sleeveless dress over my shoulder...(Photo Courtesy of Megan Mendivil)

The ALC contingent was the third in the parade. Tradition has it "The Women's Motorcycle Contingent," also known as "Dykes on Bikes" always rides first. They would be followed by "Mikes on Bikes" and then us.

I've always loved the Dykes on Bike's contingent. There were hundreds of motorcycles of every conceivable make and model, ridden by hundreds of women, sometimes in varying states of undress. What's not to love? Even watching at home on TV you get a sense of the roar of all those hundreds of engines, and it's pretty thrilling. But being within a few feet of those bikes, you could feel the roar of those engines in your gut, and it was guy heaven! So we waited our turn, and while we did I rode around checking out the big bikes, or just hung around visiting with friends from the ride. Finally, when we heard the mighty roar of all those engines racing at once, we knew we'd be going soon. I went to the front of our pack to watch the women roll out. It was an awesome sight, and if all I did was see those bikes pass, it would have well been worth coming to the parade.

Finally we started out, and we were received warmly by the crowd. Just after we began, we saw a guy with a television camera in the middle of our path, and a news anchor interviewing one of the "Mikes on Bikes." Jeanne hammed it up for the camera, waving as she rode by. I was behind her and to her side, and I was a bit surprised, because she normally tries to pretend she's pretty reserved. Jeanne swears she was just trying to signal other riders to keep them from running over the cameraman. By now though, I figure I've ridden about 2,000 miles with her, and I have yet to see that particular signal. Suffice it to say her "Don't run over the cameraman" signal looks strikingly similar to those kids you see goofing off for the news cameras behind the interviewer, when a freak newsworthy event occurs in their neighborhoods.

The crowd was huge, and I was worried there was no way we'd ever find Laurie and Megan again, but there they were. Laurie was waving like crazy, and Megan was snapping picture as quickly as my camera would let her. She took some awesome photos!

All in all, we had a great time, and it was great fun being cheered by the crowd, but way too soon it was over. Jeanne and I rode back around through some deserted streets, and eventually we were able to rejoin Laurie and Megan. The rest of the parade was wonderfully entertaining, and I can't imagine missing it ever again.

I was particularly moved by the families marching together, with signs saying "We love our queer family" or "I love my gay son" or even "I love my two moms." Conservatives always talk about the "Gay Lifestyle" but I think these families demonstrate the gay lifestyle often involves packing your kid's lunch, sending them off to school, and then heading off to work, pretty much like everybody else's lifestyle.

Interestingly enough, a week later when I showed what I considered to be the more innocuous photos of The Ride and Pride Parade to some less than gay-friendly people I know, they were appalled at the sight of these signs, and exclaimed, "how sad" and "how sick." These were simply pictures of families, with little kids for God's sake, looking just like everybody else's family, and they were still appalled! I was sickened by their reaction. So much for my theory on those more flamboyant folks (like Jeanne and I) toning it down a bit so less tolerant folks might be more accepting.

When these same people came to the picture of Jeanne and I waving to Megan and Laurie in our ribbon clad bikes and helmets, and our matching purple shirts, they did an impression of us, waving with exaggerated limp wrists, and saying "hi there" in exaggerated "gay" voices. They hadn't looked close enough at the photo to realize they were making fun of me, not that it would be any less offensive were it not me in the photo.

I'd like to thank God for giving me that brief moment to walk in another guy's shoes. It goes without saying I was (and still am) infuriated by that behavior. It's hard to believe people so backwards still exist among us.

So, back at the parade, Jeanne and I were desperate to find a bathroom, and Megan had gone through two sets of batteries in the digital camera, and needed more. Jeanne and I set out on our bikes to find both. We had no luck on the batteries, everybody was sold out, but we did find two Port-a-potties. We weren't happy, but it wasn't like we were unfamiliar with the concept.

If you haven't gathered by now, our bikes are pretty important to us. I normally don't carry a lock, because I'd never go anywhere where I might have to leave my bike out of sight. My bike is less easily replaced than my car. It sleeps in my bedroom. It's not just the value of the bike, but it takes a great deal of time to adjust the bars and the seat just perfectly, and to adjust your body to the bike.

Soon, many other people joined us in our line, and among them was one of the "Sisters of Perpetual Indulgence." These "Sisters of Perpetual Indulgence" were exactly the kind of flamboyant Pride Parade participants I was writing about earlier. These people have absolutely no right to dress so outrageously, err…like Jeanne and I, and have fun at a pride parade.

Not only do they dress colorfully, but I've since learned they raise a lot of money for such "controversial" causes as the American Cancer Society, San Francisco Suicide Prevention, and PAWS (Pets Are Wonderful Support), a group which helps low income individuals with disabling diseases, including HIV/AIDS, to keep their animals by providing animal food and litter, subsidized veterinary care, and in-home animal care such as dog walking, litter box changing, and grooming assistance.

As luck would have it Jeanne's port-a-potty number came up at the same time as mine, and we had no other trusted person with whom to leave our bikes. After all, we weren't on the ride anymore. We hadn't planned for this eventuality, and Jeanne knew exactly what I was thinking without my having to say it. She looked over at "the Sister" and said "she's a nun."

You know, somehow, it made sense, even though I know she's not really a nun. In fact, truth be told, I know she isn't really even a "she," but we trusted her with our bikes, and somehow, we knew she'd take care of them. I emerged from my port-a potty before Jeanne, and began "washing" my hands with my Purell instant hand sanitizer, still on my bike pack from the ride. The sister asked if I would mind waiting for her while she used the bathroom, so that she might use the Purell when she was done.

Jeanne emerged from her port-a-john, but by now the nun had gone in, and after Jeanne finished washing her hands, she was ready to roll. I told her I had to wait, and when the sister emerged, she washed her hands with my Purell and we chatted. She asked my name, and then introduced herself as "Sister Uma Gawd." She was warm, friendly, kind, and the end of another one of my tired ignorant notions.

Two months after the ride, Jeanne and I were once again riding around and talking about this very thing. I told her I feel like Scrooge in Dickens's Christmas Carol, because it's almost as if some ghost of ALC present has transported me from one scene to another, educating me every step of the way.

For me, there was a lot more to this journey than the 585 miles between San Francisco and Los Angeles. This journey has been about tolerance, and acceptance.

So really, this book could have been completely different. Maybe I should have written an anthropological study of the "gay lifestyle" to educate conservatives. It would have been a huge disappointment for them.

It might have gone something like this: The gay lifestyle involves family and good friends who are caring, dedicated, kind, and warm. Gay folks, and those with whom they associate, work hard, play hard, and laugh, and cry, and get emotional. It has been my observation that gay people and their friends are good to children, respectful of their elders, and kind to animals. A disproportional number of gay people and their friends ride bicycles. But without question, the major difference I see between the "gay lifestyle" and the "straight lifestyle" is gay individuals drink much more Gatorade, and, oh yeah, they wear red dresses on Thursdays.

It's funny where life might take you. I never thought I'd ride a bike across the Golden Gate Bridge, let alone to Sausalito, Tiburon, Fairfax, Lagunitas, or Petaluma.

I never dreamed I'd ride a bike to Santa Cruz or Aptos, King City, Paso Robles, Santa Maria, Lompoc, Ventura and certainly not Los Angeles.

I never thought I'd ride my bike in the San Francisco Lesbian, Gay, Bisexual, and Transgender Pride Parade. And maybe the last thing I ever thought I'd ever do in my life was share my Purell instant hand sanitizer with Sister Uma Gawd of the Sisters of Perpetual Indulgence at the San Francisco Lesbian, Gay, Bisexual, and Transgender Pride Parade.

I'm so grateful the AIDS/LifeCycle has opened all of these doors for me, and opened my eyes just a little wider. It has been such a wonderful adventure, and I know I've made a life long memory which I'll cherish forever.

Would I do it again?

I think about my fellow riders and I've seen how they've been hurt by HIV and AIDS; some of them devastated by their losses, and some nearly killed by this insidious pandemic. Many are justifiably angry. The Ride is a means of fighting back against AIDS and, at least, getting in a few good licks.

Somehow, during my journey, their fight became mine, and when they go into battle again next year, I want to be right there beside them. Well...okay...behind them.

On August 13, 2005, Jeanne and I sat at my kitchen table, filled out our registration forms for ALC 5, and sent them in.

Oh yeah...and on January 22, 2006, with the help of my bike Godmother, Shelly Ross, Jeanne and I led our first ALC training ride. Jeanne led the stretching exercises and then I gathered the group and began:

Ride defensively and always stay alert. Always assume car drivers don't see you...

The End

Thank You

There are some special folks I'd like to thank who helped me along in this journey.

First, I'd like to thank all my readers. Thank you, Duane Carlson and Carol Easter. Actually, Duane and Carol not only read my stuff and encouraged me, but also contributed generously. Oh and Duane, thank Brenda too. She probably won't read this.

I'd again like to thank all my sponsors. I'd love to name you all, but it may prove to be an inconvenience to you when folks read this and realize you're such kind, generous people and you are inundated with other people contacting you for every conceivable charity

My Father-in -law, David Saxton, doesn't have a computer. I don't know why he doesn't...he's not Amish or anything. Anyway, it was more difficult for him to follow my training progress, but he managed. He also sponsored me, but what meant even more to me was his genuine interest in this endeavor, from start to finish. David is normally an "early to bed, early to rise" kind of guy. While I was on the ride, he stayed up late every night and waited for progress reports from Laurie, after I'd call her. Thanks to you Bobbye!

Thank you so much Stephen Cadby, Chris Cole, Sherri Lunn, and the entire ALC staff. You folks are truly amazing. In my wildest dreams I could not imagine an event of this magnitude running so smoothly. Your care and dedication is obvious and I am truly grateful for the sacrifices you all have made to make The Ride happen. The love which fills this entire

261

event could only flow from the top down. Extra thanks Stephen for all of your time and effort.

Thanks to all my ALC Brother and Sister Riders and Roadies. You people made a miracle happen and you took care of me like family!

Special thanks to the Positive Pedalers for your dedication and inspiration. You are awesome!

Thank you to Shelly Ross, Bob Katz, and Larry Rachleff for photos…I swear you guys could be professionals.

And a very special Thank you to Lydia Winkeller, Shivie Cook, Lloyd (hermano mio) Carrera, Kate (the quint) Topolski, and Kelly and Tilmin Hudson, for your stories. You guys made me laugh, you made me cry, and you touched my soul.

I really need to thank all the Training Ride Leaders…some of you I was never even introduced to, but you guided me and I appreciate it. Some of you all but dragged me up hills…and I don't even know your names…the guy who swept me on "the Fateful ride of '04" is an angel (have I ever said that about a guy before?) and I never even knew his name, but after some research, I think it was Robert Manuel. The same applies to the guy who swept me on the "Sheep ride." Shelly says she remembers it being Dan Hertlein. And there are others, special folks all, and I thank you here…and I wish I could thank you all by name.

Those whom I do remember, in alphabetical order are: Ben Armstrong…how appropriate that you should be first, you worked so hard, and organized so well, and taught us all so much on those CAT II rides, (well done!), Bill Andrews (I'm a TRL now so I guess if it's okay to lie about hills, it's okay to lie about alphabetical order), Randy Barber, Bruce Bignami, Julie Brown who encouraged me to sign up, and go to my first training ride, and sang me up the Sausalito Hill on my first run,

Clay Cadic, Josie Chapman, my cycle buddy who answered all my e-mail questions in a flash, Stephanie Chenard, the doll who thinks I'm stalking her, Joseph Collins, who swept me so many times on the CAT II's and was ready to fight for me when some thug tried to run me into traffic, Debra Darlington, Edna Flores, who played Brady bunch trivial pursuit with Megan, Jeanne, and me, George Harrison, my first face-to-face contact and a saint, Valdez Hill, The Hudsen sisters, Kelly and Tilman, Nick Johnson, Bob Katz, a wealth of information and one of my first Training Ride Leaders, and I think Jeanne still owes him a tube, SuperDave Kim, Alan Kwok, who cheered us up so many hills, and a young man who I have truly grown to love as he brings nothing but good to the world, Sue Lackey, my friend and hand gesturer extraordinaire, Tammy Lovlie, Robert Manual, Derek Martin, Cynthia McCool, Ian Menzies, Susan Parish, who signed me up, Evelyn Rogerson, Dita Rudinow, Raul (Rowdy)Torres, Tai Trang, Lydia Winkeller, the most beautiful woman I ever avoided, and another who really encouraged me from the beginning, even though I didn't actually meet her until much, much later.

And yeah, I went out of order again here, Shelly Ross, Thank you! You taught me more about riding, and The Ride than anyone. You introduced me to so many people and so much fun. I followed you like a lost pup in the beginning, and I will never forget all you've done for me. You are my bike Godmother, and I know the only way I can ever pay you back is to help someone else along...but I could never do it as well as you.

So now that I'm done thanking the Ride Leaders, there's still Jeanne, with whom I have ridden more than a couple of thousand miles. We know each other so well I can tell whether we're turning left or right, slowing or stopping by the way your ass twitches, and that's just too many miles. We've shared food and drink, tears and laughter, and of course, butt butter and gossip. What a joy it has been to ride with you, and grow a friendship with you! I'm sure we'll be riding for many years to come. Thank you for being my family on the road. You've made the miles so much easier, and so much fun! Thanks for teaching me it takes funny to know funny, and so many other things. Thank you for all your help with the book too! I look forward to many more thousands of miles of suffering together. Love ya, bitch!

Thanks to my Mom and Dad for everything…and I do mean everything. Thanks to my Sibs Rick and Vickie and Demi and David for your support. We are so fortunate that we all have each other.

Thanks Sarah Marie for making the book a realistic possibility.

Thanks to my daughters, Erin, Megan, and Katelyn. Thanks for listening to my stories over and over. Thanks for checking my grammar. Thanks for being a joy to rear, thanks for keeping me entertained, and for giving me the pride of knowing I had a small part in raising three of the finest young women on earth. I love you guys!

And way too often last, but never least, I want to thank my wife Laurie. Without her I doubt I'd even be alive, forget doing a ride like this. Thank you for sharing my life, the longest, hardest, biggest and sweetest adventure of them all with me. Thanks for sticking with me through sickness, and nursing me back to health. Thanks for waking up every single morning with me, no matter how early, making me oatmeal and coffee and sending me on my way with a kiss and an "I love you."

Thanks for never saying "you're riding again!?" Thanks for encouraging me, and never doubting me, and for making me believe I can do anything. Thanks for helping me all the way through, but to take a week of vacation just to get me ready was way above and beyond. They say behind every great man there's a great woman, sometimes that's true of even mediocre men! I could never thank you enough, and I will never say I love you enough for you to know how much I mean it.

ALC fundraising rule #1…It never hurts to ask!

If you read this book and are so moved, I'd really appreciate it if you'd go to:

www.aidslifecycle.org/homepage/

Then just type in my name on the search…that's right…that's R-U-S-S-E-L-L. Last name's M-E-N-D-I-V-I-L. Then…click on search for participant…then click on my name. That will direct you to my homepage where you can show your generosity and support. Every donation helps. It doesn't have to be a big donation, though I like those too. This is a really great cause or else I wouldn't be riding my bike 585 miles…again. Please leave a message so I know who you are, and an e-mail so I can write.

If I'm not listed, maybe my legs fell off, or I died, or maybe one of my kids was graduating from college and I had to miss the ride that year, or if you just don't like me (it could happen!?), you can look up any one of the names in this book the same way. They'll probably be riding again too.

Heck, you can just pick a name at random and they'll probably be a really good person, and you can sponsor them. Really! I've yet to meet a jerk affiliated in any way with this ride.

And if you want to ride, if you're even considering it, you can do it! I did it, and I'm a big fat guy with a two heart attack history. And if you do it...you have my word on this...you won't regret it...ever. Your ass will hate you for it...but I promise you, this will be an amazing experience which you will cherish for the rest of your life. Maybe just try out a training ride...

www.aidslifecycle.org

Thanks again,

Russ

Printed in the United States
132763LV00003B/52-111/A